THE
HUMANITY

THE FUTURE OF HUMANITY

REVELATION 4 TO 22 / MURRAY ROBERTSON

AN ALBATROSS BOOK

the bible reading fellowship
OPENING THE BIBLE

© Commentary: Murray Robertson 1993
© Discussion questions: Albatross Books Pty Ltd 1993

Published in Australia and New Zealand by
Albatross Books Pty Ltd
PO Box 320, Sutherland
NSW 2232, Australia
in the United States of America by
Albatross Books
PO Box 131, Claremont
CA 91711, USA
and in the United Kingdom by
Lion Publishing plc
Peter's Way, Sandy Lane West
Oxford OX4 5HG, England

First edition 1993

*This book is copyright. Apart from any fair
dealing for the purposes of private study,
research, criticism or review as permitted
under the Copyright Act, no part of this book
may be reproduced by any process without
the written permission of the publisher.*

National Library of Australia
Cataloguing-in-Publication data

Robertson, Murray
The Future of Humanity
ISBN 0 7324 1019 3 (Albatross)
ISBN 0 7459 2443 3 (BRF)

1. Bible. N.T. Revelation — Commentaries. I. Title

228.07

Cover photo: John Waterhouse
Printed and bound in Australia by Griffin Paperbacks, Netley, SA

Contents

Introduction   7

1 The saga of human history
REVELATION CHAPTER 4, VERSE 1 TO
CHAPTER 7, VERSE 17   24

2 The saga of life on the earth
REVELATION CHAPTER 8, VERSE 1 TO
CHAPTER 11, VERSE 18   54

3 The church and the powers
REVELATION CHAPTER 11, VERSE 19 TO
CHAPTER 15, VERSE 4   77

4 The road to Armageddon
REVELATION CHAPTER 15, VERSE 5 TO
CHAPTER 16, VERSE 21   111

5 The system that seduces the world
REVELATION CHAPTER 17, VERSE 1 TO
CHAPTER 19, VERSE 10   124

6 The final horseman
REVELATION CHAPTER 19, VERSE 11 TO
CHAPTER 20, VERSE 15   148

7 Beyond the end of time
REVELATION CHAPTER 21, VERSE 1 TO
CHAPTER 22, VERSE 21   165

Endnotes   185
Bibliography   188

Introduction

FOR MANY, REVELATION IS A CLOSED BOOK. It seems filled with obscure visions and difficult-to-understand passages. Yet it is the final word from the ascended Lord to his followers. Its message inspired great hope among the early Christians. And wherever its message has been understood, Christian communities have faced the future with hope.

This book speaks to us about the future of the human race. It tells us of the power of prayer to bring about change in the world. It is a word of encouragement to suffering believers to stay faithful to their Lord. It is a word of celebration that Jesus, who once suffered and died on the cross, now reigns at the right hand of God and one day will return in power and glory. It is a word of prophetic challenge. God promises that he will stand on the side of the oppressed, the persecuted and the poor, and that he will act on their behalf, both through and at the end of history.

Today 'end times' preachers offer an alternative way to understand Revelation. Crowds flock to hear the book of Revelation being promoted as a code book that refers to a period in history far removed from the time when John was given this revelation. This book, we are told, refers to specific events in our own day. People sit open-mouthed at the ability of such preachers to find hidden meanings in the text. We are told that a great evil is coming on the world, but there is little we can do about it. We are to flee from getting involved with the world and watch for signs of the onset of terrible judgments — because, before they happen, those who follow Jesus will be taken away and will not have to suffer.

In 1989, I preached a series of messages on the book of Revelation. They were momentous days. The Berlin Wall fell as tides of freedom and liberty were flowing throughout eastern Europe. It was very interesting to be looking at the message of Revelation at the same time as these events were happening. However, I noticed a disconcerting trend. Several people who normally worship with us didn't appear as I began the series on Revelation. When I asked some why they stayed away, it transpired they had previously been scared by 'end times' preachers. Rather than hearing a call to prophetic involvement in the world, they had been told that awful things would happen about which they could do nothing. One or two had suffered nightmares as a consequence.

I am sure the apostle John would have been horrified at this response to his message of hope. His purpose was to write a prophetic word revealing God's purposes for his people. It is consistent with the message of the Old Testament prophets. It is consistent with what we read in the Gospels. God has always had a purpose for the world and has always called people to be involved with him in it.

Faulty ways to interpret Revelation

Let us look at three ways of interpreting Revelation which I believe are not correct.

❏ *The first faulty way is to identify particular passages in Revelation with specific world events and people.*

An example is the number 666. In Revelation 13, we read that people will bear what is called the 'mark of the beast', which is the number 666. A few years ago a popular Bible teacher said that the Australian credit card, Bankcard, bore the mark of the beast. How? There is a stylised 'b' on the card and it is in three different colours so, if we use our imaginations, we can see the number 666!

Another example is the identity of the antichrist. Lenin, Stalin, Hitler, Mussolini, Mao Tse Tung and Pol Pot have all been candidates in the twentieth century. All are dead or off the world stage. There is no doubt that there have been terrible tyrants in this and past centuries. In their denial of individual freedom, their appalling cruelty and their defiance of God, they all give expression to the power of the antichrist. However, there is real danger in identifying each successive despot who struts his stuff as the final manifestation of the antichrist and the sign of the end of the age.

But getting the details wrong is not the only problem. What is also wrong with this approach is that we can easily become passive, overwhelmed with the feeling that the world is slipping out of control. Bankcards are being issued, soon we will have the number 666 on our foreheads, the anti-christ is about to strike — and we can do nothing about it. But this conclusion is the *opposite* of the message of the biblical prophets. The prophets in the Old Testament, after they had told their hearers the things that would happen, did not then say, 'There is nothing we can do; the world is going to get worse and worse; all we can do is wait for God to step in — and watch it happen.' Although at times they prophesied that the most appalling evils would engulf the world, they called on people to make an intelligent response, to align themselves on the side of God and become involved in the struggle against evil, oppression and injustice.

Largely because of the faulty popular emphasis

outlined here, there is a fatalism and fear in parts of the Christian community today. But this fatalism is a denial of Christian hope. If we get sick, we do not think, 'I am going to die one day and when I die I'm going to meet the Lord, so I will just sit back and wait — there is nothing I can do.' There is a lot we can do. We can go to a doctor, we can get people to pray for us, we can undertake to improve our health by a proper diet and exercise program. Sickness is an evil we are called to fight.

We need to be careful when we hear people preaching on Revelation. We need to know how they are calling us to respond. Is it basically to speculate and draw up charts — and wait for it all to happen? Or does it lead us to involvement in the world, a costly discipleship and participation in the suffering of others? If the former, then what is being offered is not authentic biblical Christianity, but escapism. This is the measure of a true understanding of biblical prophecy — that God is calling us to prayer and to engagement in the world against evil, injustice and oppression wherever we find it. We are called to be agents of God's healing and reconciling love in the world, not passive voyeurs chronicling its destruction.

❏ *A second faulty way to interpret Revelation is to think of it as a calendar or chronological countdown to the last days.*

Under this method of interpretation, we start off in chapter 1 in year one and, by the time we get to chapter 22, we are in 1999 or whenever we consider the end is going to be. One man touring New Zealand a few years ago announced that Jesus was coming back in 1988. I don't know if he has recanted, but I notice he still gets a following!

This kind of emphasis actually brings the faith into disrepute. Jesus himself said in Mark 13, verse 32 that no-one knows the day nor the hour, only the Father in heaven. We are told to beware of people who say they know when Jesus will be back — because only the Father knows that and he hasn't told us! In any case, as we shall see, Revelation is actually constructed differently. It is not strictly a chronological account of the future, but a series of overlapping visions.

❏ *A third faulty way to interpret Revelation is to think of it as a closed book, of no relevance to our times.*

This is the opposite of those who would project the book of Revelation into the future. Here, we relegate Revelation to a dim and dusty past. When the Reformer Martin Luther drew up his own canon of New Testament scripture, there were some books he didn't like, so he left them out. He didn't include Revelation in his New Testament because, he said, it was an obscure writing, with threats of disobedience when no-one could understand what was being said![1]

This assessment is in marked contrast to another view that states that Revelation is the only masterpiece of pure art in the New Testament — it is beautiful beyond description.[2]

Keys to understanding Revelation

I believe there is a way to understand Revelation which makes sense of what is going on in the world and yet respects the integrity of the book as a coherent piece of literature and part of the New Testament canon. There are several keys which aid this understanding.

❏ *The first key is to recognise the time and the circumstances in which it was written.*

To whom did John write and why? It is very important that we understand the *context* of the original letter — it will help us understand its meaning.

It is a letter written towards the end of the first century AD by the apostle John to seven churches in Asia Minor. Its purpose is to *comfort* the persecuted church against the forces of evil and to *encourage* Christians to endure.

This message in a nutshell is: God knows what is happening — and is in control! Satan may look as though he is winning. In reality, he is mortally wounded and is under judgment. Right at the beginning of the letter in Revelation 1, verses 3 and 4, a blessing is promised from God to those people in the seven churches who read it.

Now, if everything in Revelation only related to things that were to happen hundreds of years in the future, it would have made fairly tedious listening. It would have made no sense to those who heard it — they certainly would not have received any clear message or positive call to action for their time. Whatever the book of Revelation means to us today, it must have meant something to John's original readers, otherwise why read it?

In some situations when the early Christians came together to worship, they had no idea from one Sunday to the next who would be there the following week. In the Roman Empire, if you were a Christian, you could die for your faith — just as is the case in many parts of the world today if you openly confess your faith in Jesus Christ. In this context, the message made sense to those first readers. So any interpretation of this book today must be one that would also have made sense to them.

❑ *The second key is that Revelation is a series of visions, describing the same events but from a different perspective, each deepening in significance.*
Revelation is not strictly a chronological sequence of events, as if we have to try and fit every incident into a timetable. It isn't a literal calendar at all. What is being dealt with in Revelation is so far beyond the

realm of human experience that it had to be presented in some appropriate manner. It's not like the Gospels or the writings of Paul, where we can find literal accounts of specific historical events.

In Revelation we are told in seven different ways, in seven series of visions, essentially the same thing. Throughout the earth, between the first coming of Jesus and the second, certain things will happen. Then Jesus will return in power and glory to wind up history as we know it and the whole universe will see that Jesus Christ is Lord. However, those committed to the idea that Revelation describes a fixed sequence of events end up with a headache, because it is so difficult to fit the visions together in chronological order.

❏ *The third key is that the pictures used in the vision are symbolic.*

Symbol is the language of vision. The beautiful woman, the whore, the four horsemen are not necessarily actual people. They are descriptive of and represent events, situations and movements in history.

Each vision begins with life as it was after Jesus' ascension and ends with judgment falling on earth — or a scene of triumph in heaven. As we move through the book, the visions increase in intensity, until we reach the final judgment.

In the centuries prior to John's revelation, many others had visions of the future. The writings of

Some Common Symbols used in Revelation

Sealed scroll (or book) = God's unfinished plan for the age

Eyes = intellectual penetration

Lion = strength
Man = intelligence
Ox = service
Eagle = swiftness
(see 4: 6–7)

Number four is associated with four directions of the world (e.g. four angels of 7: 1 = messengers to control the wind)

Number seven = number of completeness

Number six = number of incompleteness

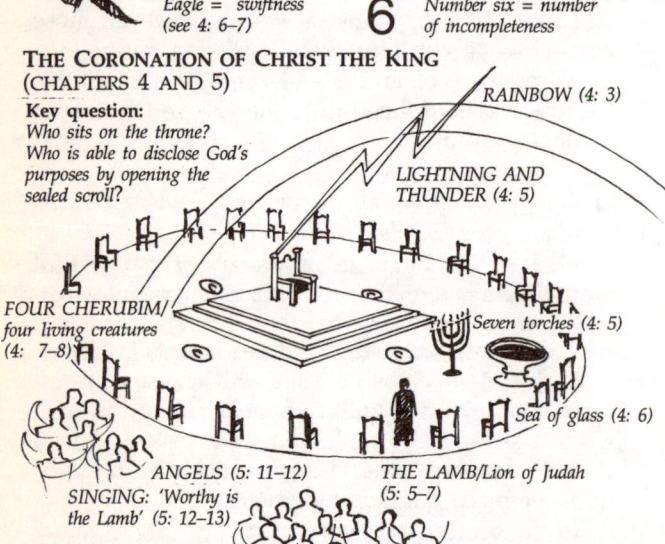

The Coronation of Christ the King
(Chapters 4 and 5)

Key question:
Who sits on the throne?
Who is able to disclose God's purposes by opening the sealed scroll?

RAINBOW (4: 3)

LIGHTNING AND THUNDER (4: 5)

FOUR CHERUBIM/four living creatures (4: 7–8)

Seven torches (4: 5)

Sea of glass (4: 6)

ANGELS (5: 11–12)

THE LAMB/Lion of Judah (5: 5–7)

SINGING: 'Worthy is the Lamb' (5: 12–13)

Twenty four elders represent: twelve tribes of Israel (saints of old covenant), twelve apostles (saints of new covenant)

Scene = an ornamental throne room with a raised dais in middle. All the details are to reinforce the impression of God's majesty and might.

those who saw these things became known as 'apocalyptic' literature. Within the literature various symbols can be found, which seem to have had a common usage and understanding. Beasley-Murray suggests that the closest modern parallel is the political cartoon.[3] The cartoonist employs symbols. Some of those are human like John Bull and Uncle Sam. Others are animals like the British lion, the Russian bear and the American eagle. At our period of history, they are readily understood. Similarly, the use of numbers, animals, people and other symbols in the book of Revelation would have been readily understood by John's contemporaries.

The early Christians to whom John was writing understood what he was writing about in a way that the church may have subsequently lost, because it often stopped experiencing visions and prophetic words. The church today has the potential to understand more clearly what John was writing about because, in the last couple of decades, we have been rediscovering the way the Holy Spirit speaks to us in visions. This is not to suggest that any vision today has the same authority as the biblical visions. But being in a situation where these things happen does help us appreciate the nature of visionary experience.

❏ *The last and undoubtedly the most important key is that it is Jesus on the cross who is central to our understanding of history.*

This point is made clearly in chapter 5, verses 1 to 14. The cross is the revelation to humanity of the nature of God. God has revealed himself to us as someone who loves and cares for us enough to take on our humanity, to suffer and to die. Not only that, but the cross is also the pattern for our discipleship a calling to take up the cross and to follow Jesus; to become a servant, bringing God's healing love to the world, identifying with the poor, the lost and the oppressed.

The message of Revelation is that we are called to live a lifestyle consistent with the kingdom that Jesus will establish — a kingdom of justice, righteousness, freedom and joy. We are not called to be passive or fearful — we are called to be involved in the world, spreading the gospel of the kingdom. Injustice, oppression, famine and death are evils. They are not part of God's intention for this planet and we are called to be active in the struggle against them. *That* is what Jesus did — and he is the key to human history and the key to understanding this book.

Discussion questions

Talking it through

1 Many contemporary Bible teachers like to apply the message of Revelation to specific political events.
   (a) What view of the future does much of the 'mark of the beast' thinking contain?
   (b) What effect does this thinking have on us? Do you see this as helpful?

2 'Revelation is primarily aimed at people's attitudes to the present.' Do you agree? What is your supporting argument?

3 'Fatalism is a denial of Christian hope.' How does fatalism affect our attitude to life? How does fatalism actually promote the triumph of evil?

4 Why, do you think, is the second coming of Jesus so important to the writer of the Book of Revelation? Is it a doctrine that has appeal to certain generations over others —

or the church in particular societies? Which ones? Why?

5 Think about the worldwide persecution of Christians in the world today.
   (a) Are their experiences isolated ones, or are they in some way inextricably linked? How?
   (b) Christians in the West have not really suffered for their faith, unlike their brethren in the former USSR, China, Africa, South America and (increasingly) the Muslim countries of the world. We are also materially better off than our Third World Christians. Is there a connection?

Widening our horizons

1 Examine each of the following statements, deciding whether or not you agree and why:
  (a) 'Human beings are getting worse and worse. We are on the slow, inexorable decline into social chaos.'
  (b) 'God is going to blow the whistle soon. Things are so bad that he's just *got* to act.'
  (c) 'Things are as they've always been — humankind is no better or no worse than in times past.'
  (d) 'There are definite signs that the world is a better place to live in than it ever has been. Look at the breakthroughs in medical science, computer technology, urban planning! The world is a safer and happier place for our children.'
  (e) 'Communism is the history of man's inhumanity to man. With capitalism, it is just the other way round!'
  What is *your* attitude to the future?
How does this affect your attitude to the present?

2 Answer the following questions about one extra-sensory experience you might have had: a vision, a significant dream, a compelling sense of hearing a message and so on.
  (a) Why do you think you received it? What has it shown you about yourself?
  (b) What feeling did it leave you with? Was it beneficial at the time?
  (c) What long-term effect did it have on you? How have you been able to incorporate it into your experience of life generally?
  (d) Do you see it as having come from God? Why/Why not?

3 Symbols, in Revelation as well as elsewhere, often convey more than words. What does each of these symbols mean:
  (a) The hammer and sickle?
  (b) A clenched fist?
  (c) Arms held wide towards someone?
  (d) The cross?
  Do you feel that a symbol is more or less powerful than words?

4 What do you imagine God might say to us about each of the following:
  (a) The tough time the poor are having in

our society?
(b) The social and economic disorder in the former Soviet Union?
(c) The oppression of the disadvantaged in Latin America?
(d) The sense of cynicism and hopelessness often shown by the young?

Does the Christian church have a particular duty to respond to these needs, or are they more the job of governments?

5 Write a short prayer for one of the above problem areas in the world today (listed in question 4). Alternatively, have each member write a short prayer on each and share them together.

1
The saga of human history

REVELATION CHAPTER 4, VERSE 1 TO
CHAPTER 7, VERSE 17

❧

THE FIRST THREE CHAPTERS of the book of Revelation are relatively easy to understand. John has been imprisoned for his faith on the island of Patmos — off the western coast of modern-day Turkey. While he is there, Jesus appears to him in the midst of the seven lampstands in overwhelming power and majesty. He reassures John, telling him that he is giving him a message for the seven churches of Asia Minor.

These seven letters, given in Revelation 2 and 3, are messages of encouragement and correction to each of the churches in turn.

Then, in chapters 4 and 5, begins the first vision. The rest of the book of Revelation may be summarised as follows (a diagram showing how each vision builds on the other is over the page):

VISION 1: *The coronation in heaven, the book with seven seals* (chapters 4 to 7)
VISION 2: *The seven trumpets of judgment* (chapters 8 to 11)
VISION 3: *The woman and the male child persecuted by the dragon and his helpers, the beast and the harlot* (chapters 12 to 14)
VISION 4: *The seven bowls of wrath* (chapters 15 and 16)
VISION 5: *The woman on the beast, the fall of the harlot and the beast* (chapters 17 to 19)
VISION 6: *The white horse, the 1000-year reign, the final judgment and the defeat of the dragon* (chapters 19 and 20)
VISION 7: *The new heaven and earth; the new Jerusalem* (chapters 21 and 22).

The vision of the throne of God
(chapter 4, verses 1 to 11)

John in this vision finds himself standing before an open door in heaven, with Jesus speaking to him again. John is given, for the benefit of the rest of humanity, an insight into what is actually happening at the very centre of the universe.

THE STRUCTURE OF THE BOOK OF REVELATION

Misinterpretations of the book of Revelation abound because people read the book wrongly. Revelation is not a straight chronological account, but is rather a series of seven *parallel visions*, each building on the other. Each vision is looking at the same events, but from a different perspective.

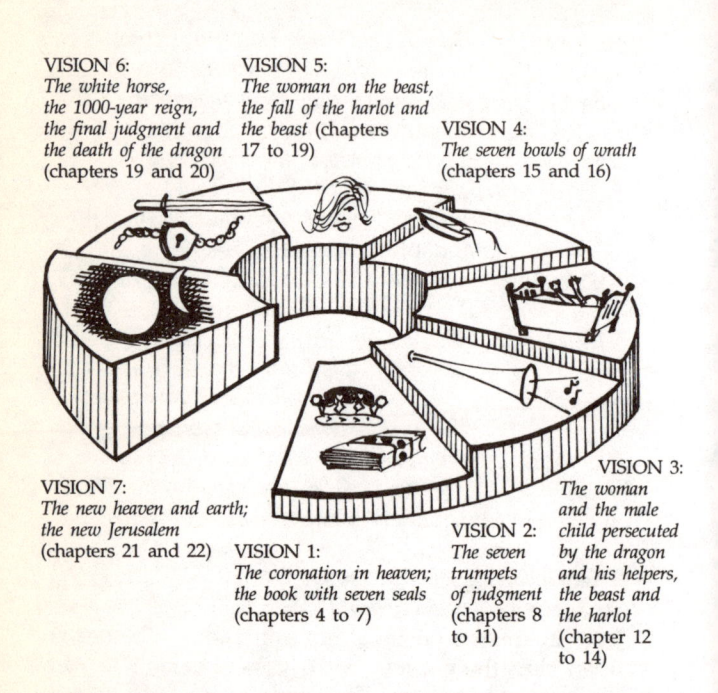

VISION 6:
The white horse, the 1000-year reign, the final judgment and the death of the dragon (chapters 19 and 20)

VISION 5:
The woman on the beast, the fall of the harlot and the beast (chapters 17 to 19)

VISION 4:
The seven bowls of wrath (chapters 15 and 16)

VISION 7:
The new heaven and earth; the new Jerusalem (chapters 21 and 22)

VISION 1:
The coronation in heaven; the book with seven seals (chapters 4 to 7)

VISION 2:
The seven trumpets of judgment (chapters 8 to 11)

VISION 3:
The woman and the male child persecuted by the dragon and his helpers, the beast and the harlot (chapter 12 to 14)

Each vision deepens in significance, as each vision gets closer to the ultimate question: 'What happens when the trumpet blasts and human history, as we now know it, is wrapped up for all time? What happens at the last judgment?' The reader is kept waiting until the last chapters!

There is a widespread conviction today that nothing is at the centre of the universe. A problem for modern science is why, at a given point at a certain time, a universe should have come into existence at all if, in fact, there is no creator and everything happens by random chance. 'Why should the universe go to all the bother of existing?' asks Stephen Hawking.[1] John is given the revelation that the creator, and his throne, are at the centre of the universe. The universe *does* have meaning — and it has a future.

Around God is the most amazing sight. John sees a throne and over the throne is a rainbow. We first meet the rainbow in Genesis 9, verses 13 to 17. After the earth had been judged through the flood, God said he would never again flood the earth, giving humanity a sign, the rainbow. God is saying through the sign of a rainbow over his throne that peace has been declared between God and ourselves.

Around the throne are four strange characters whom John calls 'the four living creatures'. These creatures appear elsewhere in the scriptures. Ezekiel saw them, or something very like them, when God appeared to him on one occasion (Ezekiel 1). It seems most likely that they are non-human, created beings.

Each of the four living creatures has six wings and is covered with eyes even under his wings. What are they doing? They have one function: their task is to worship God for all eternity. Around them, as they worship God and declare God's greatness, is a circle of twenty-four elders. Every time the living creatures start blessing and praising God, these twenty-four elders prostrate themselves and they worship God, too.

This is a symbol, the twenty-four elders referring to the twelve tribes of Israel and the twelve apostles of Jesus representing the saints of the old covenant and of the new. It must be symbolic because one of the apostles was actually standing there watching the whole scene — including himself! We see here a picture of the unity of the people of God over the whole earth. All the people who have faithfully followed God right through human history are here surrounding the throne of God and worshipping him.

Why does God tell us to worship him all the time? Is God an egotist? Why is it that at the centre of the universe these created beings, who represent the whole of God's creation, are worshipping God? Why does God need all these worshipping beings? Why are we also told to praise God? C.S. Lewis is very helpful on this. In his book *Reflections on the Psalms*, he says:

> The most obvious fact about praise — whether of God or anything — strangely escaped me. I thought of it in terms of compliment, approval, or the giving of honour. I had never noticed that all enjoyment spontaneously overflows into praise

unless (sometimes even if) shyness or the fear of boring others is deliberately brought in to check it. . .

I had not noticed how the humblest and at the same time most balanced and capacious minds praised most, while the cranks, misfits and malcontents praised least. . . Except where intolerably adverse circumstances interfere, praise almost seems to be inner health made audible. . .

I had not noticed either that just as men spontaneously praise whatever they value, so they spontaneously urge us to join them in praising it: 'Isn't she lovely?' 'Wasn't it glorious?' 'Don't you think that magnificent?' The Psalmists in telling everyone to praise God are doing what all men do when they speak of what they care about.

My whole, more general, difficulty about the praise of God depended on my absurdly denying to us, as regards the supremely valuable, what we delight to do, what indeed we can't help doing, about everything else we value. I think we delight to praise what we enjoy because the praise not merely expresses but completes the enjoyment; it is its appointed consummation. It is not out of compliment that lovers keep on telling one another how beautiful they are; the delight is incomplete till it is expressed.[2]

The vision of the scroll
(chapter 5, verses 1 to 14)

John saw a scroll in God's right hand. We find, as the story goes on, that the scroll is the saga of human history, of God's unfinished purposes for his creation. In chapter 6, we will see how this scroll begins to be unrolled and the whole of human history starts to play itself out. But who, amongst all God's created beings, is worthy to open the scroll that contains the key to all human history? John tells us that he wept because nobody was good enough to undo the scroll. Then someone says, 'Do not weep. See, the Lion of the tribe of Judah, the Root of David, has conquered, so that he can open the scroll and its seven seals.' John looks around and, instead of seeing a lion, he sees a lamb. It is Jesus, the Lamb who once was slain.

This Lamb has seven horns, the symbol of power, and seven eyes, meaning he is all-seeing. He is the one who sent the Spirit into the world. The Lamb who was slain is not just the suffering Messiah who died on the cross; he is also the risen King. John's vision moves through time to the coronation moment of the universe. The Lamb ascends the throne and takes the scroll, and all the created beings begin to worship, not just God the Father, but Jesus the Lamb who was slain.

Our prayers are also part of the process. These creatures have bowls full of incense which are the prayers of all God's people. Why are they worshipping Jesus? Because, we are told, he has purchased his people — 'ransomed for God saints from every tribe and language and people and nation' (verse 9). This is the climactic moment of human history.

Then John expresses his awe at the whole scene as a vast number of angels join with the whole of redeemed creation to worship and praise Jesus (verse 12). In Philippians 2, verses 9 to 11, Paul provides a similar picture:

> . . .and being found in human form,
> he humbled himself
> and became obedient to the point of death —
> even death on a cross.
> Therefore God also highly exalted him
> and gave him the name
> that is above every name,
> so that at the name of Jesus
> every knee should bend,
> in heaven and on earth and under the earth,
> and every tongue confess
> that Jesus Christ is Lord,
> to the glory of God the Father.

There is a day coming when Jesus will be worshipped, praised and glorified. What John is saying is remarkable because, when he wrote Revelation, the Christians were a tiny scattered handful of persecuted people. He is saying that the man who died on the cross is, in fact, the key to human history.

John could not possibly have known that, in the two thousand years that followed, this one man who hung on the cross would have more impact on humankind than any other man who has ever lived. Millions of people all over the world give allegiance to this man. This is the man who has inspired countless thousands to give their lives for the poor of the earth. This is the man who holds the key to human history — and God in his grace and goodness allows us to know about him, to love him and one day to gather around the throne and praise him.

THE FIRST SEAL: *the white horse*
(chapter 6, verses 1 and 2)

John watches as Jesus breaks the first seal, and he sees a white horse (verse 2). Who is the first horseman? Is this Jesus himself? We get *another* description of a man riding a white horse in chapter 19, verse 11:

> Then I saw heaven opened, and there was a white horse! Its rider is called Faithful and True, and in righteousness he judges and makes war. His eyes are like a flame of fire, and on his head are many diadems and he has a name inscribed that no one knows but himself. He is clothed in a robe dipped in blood, and his name is called the Word of God.

There are plenty of clues in this description. The

rider of this white horse is Jesus, the risen triumphant Lord. He has come in answer to the cries of the people of the earth for justice.

But what about Revelation 6, verse 2? Is the rider on this white horse Jesus? There are some similarities, but there are some differences as well. To resolve our difficulties, we need to look at the passage in the Gospels (Matthew 24, verses 4 to 7) where Jesus spoke of what was to come.

When we are wondering about how to interpret the symbols of Revelation, the soundest principle is to turn first to those passages of scripture that speak in a non-symbolic way of things that are dealt with through symbols in Revelation. There are, of course, nearly as many interpretations of some of the symbols as there are commentators on the passage. But following this principle and interpretation can hopefully keep us from some of the more bizarre understandings offered over the years. 'The Revelation sequence is the subject of our enquiry, and the Matthew sequence will be our control,' says Michael Wilcock.[3]

Turning to the discourse in Matthew, we note remakable parallels to what John sees in Revelation 6. In Matthew's account, Jesus was asked about the end of the age and he answered:

> Beware that no one leads you astray. For many will come in my name, saying 'I am the Messiah!' and they will lead you astray. And you will

hear of wars and rumours of wars; see that you
are not alarmed; for this must take place, but the
end is not yet. For nation will rise against nation, and kingdom against kingdom, and there
will be famines and earthquakes in various
places: all this is but the beginning of the
birthpangs.

Here Jesus refers to the same things that John saw in his vision. He talks about war, famine, death and destruction. These will be the characteristics of the age which was to come, which will last through until his return. The first thing, he says, is that many will come in his name claiming to be the Christ and they will deceive many. This suggests that the first horseman, according to the sequence that Jesus gives us, is the false Christ.

So the first sign of this age is that, alongside the suffering Messiah who is the risen King, there will be deceivers. They look something like Jesus and people can be taken in. The apostle John wrote about this in his letter when he said, 'Children, it is the last hour! As you have heard that antichrist is coming, so now many antichrists have come' (1 John 2, verse 18).

THE SECOND SEAL: *the red horse*
(chapter 6, verses 3 and 4)

The second horseman rides out on a fiery red horse. This horse is War. War will be one of the characteristic signs of the age between the first and second coming of Jesus. But how are we to understand war if we are a follower of the Prince of Peace?

There are passages in the Old Testament that make it quite clear that, when Israel went out to wage war, God fought for them. Often in the Old Testament, when the people of Israel went out to fight, a miracle occurred. The walls of Jericho fell down and the army went in — God won the victory for them. We find interesting passages like the one in Deuteronomy 20, verses 1 to 9 where the people were told not to worry if their armies were inferior to the opposition because God would be on their side. They had to put their trust in God.

There are other passages that make it quite clear that the people of God were not to put their trust in military might. For example, the prophet Isaiah said, 'Alas for those... who trust in chariots because they are many' (Isaiah 31, verse 1). Why not trust them? After all, chariots were high-tech, state-of-the-art military machines.

There is a fascinating passage in Zechariah 9, verse 9 about the Messiah riding on a donkey: 'Rejoice greatly, O Daughter of Zion! Shout aloud, O Daughter of Jerusalem! Lo, your king comes to you; triumphant and victorious is he, humble and riding on a donkey, on a colt, the foal of a donkey.' Straight after that, in verse 10, it says: 'He will cut off the chariot from Ephraim and the war horse from

Jerusalem; and the battle bow shall be cut off, and he shall command peace to the nations; his dominion shall be from sea to sea, and from the River to the ends of the earth.' In other words, when the Messiah comes, he is going to destroy the chariots, and he is going to lead his followers to put their trust, not in high-tech war machines, but in himself. The Messiah, when he comes, will be a peacemaker.

For three centuries, Christians undermined the values of the Roman Empire by their commitment to a lifestyle of non-violence. There are many recorded instances of Christians who refused to kill, even in war, and who died because of it. Christians resisted the state in non-violent ways and went to the lions. It was only after the Roman Emperor Constantine professed to be a Christian that a justification for engaging in war was developed. This depended on the cause and means of the war being just, and on war being a last resort.

Occasionally a group of Christians refuse to accept this position. Anabaptists in the sixteenth century were committed to non-violence — and they were often killed because of it. The task of the Messiah is peacemaking. Whether that justifies Christians taking up arms to go to war will continue to be a subject of debate in the Christian community. But the source of war is clear. It is the rider on the red horse.

THE THIRD SEAL: *the black horse*
(chapter 6, verses 5 and 6)

The third horseman rides a black horse and this is Famine: 'A quart of wheat for a day's wages, and three quarts of barley for a day's pay' (verse 6). Wheat was for the rich, but the cheaper barley was the poor man's fare. In John's time, you could buy sixteen quarts of wheat with a day's wages. Now, instead of getting sixteen quarts of wheat for a day's wages, you could only get one quart.

What we have is a description of severe economic scarcity. Both wheat and barley are available — but at a price.

But right in the middle of this widespread famine, we have a fascinating comment: 'Do not damage the oil and the wine' (verse 6). They were luxuries! In other words, the masses are subject to famine, but a few continue to live in plenty. This is to be a characteristic of life between the two comings of Jesus.

One of the biggest issues in the world of the 1990s is the appalling gap between the rich and the poor. At the end of the 1980s, for every one dollar of aid given by Western countries to some of the poorest countries of the Third World, Western banks collected back two dollars in interest on loans. There is seemingly no way these poorest-of-the-poor nations can get out of the appalling situation they find themselves in.

The resources of the world today are being fed

38/The saga of human history

to the red horse and millions are dying by the advance of the black horse. Pope John Paul II has said: 'The arms race kills without firing a shot.'[4] A large proportion of the huge resources of the Western world have been going into armaments. The world could sustain a much larger percentage of the world's population than it now does. We have the resources and we have the technology, but we do not have the will. What will future generations say when they look back on us? What would Amos say if he walked into the world today and saw this huge gap between the rich and the poor — and those who stand to profit in the West saying, 'Don't touch the oil and the wine. These are our luxuries. We want them intact.'?

As Christians, what do we do? Some see these things happening in the world and say, 'Aha, famine! This is one of the signs of the end. Jesus must be coming back soon.' And they wait for him to come and take them away. But is that *all* we are called to do? Jesus expects a counter-insurgency movement mounted against these horsemen. The gospel, he says, is to be preached in the whole world (Matthew 24, verse 14). Christians at their best have always been at the forefront of those working for peace and alongside the starving. This is not a negation of our conviction that Jesus is coming back. It is a response to our calling to live today by the values of that kingdom which will be revealed in its fullness at the end of time.

THE FOURTH SEAL: *the pale horse*
(chapter 6, verses 7 to 8)

The fourth horseman rides on a pale horse. He is Death — and Hades is following close behind. 'They were given authority over a fourth of the earth to kill with sword, famine and pestilence, and by the wild animals of the earth.' This is another continuing characteristic of this age.

What did the early Christians do in the face of the challenge of these four horsemen? Did they simply say, 'So be it. God has revealed that this is what is going to happen, so let's try to spot these things as they occur'? No. They fought the horsemen — even for the second one, war, which they fought by refusing to fight.

They fought the fourth horseman, premature death. The early Christians were for life. The killing of the weak and powerless, by abortion and infanticide, was eliminated from the Roman Empire through the efforts of Christians who refused to lie down and let these horsemen ride roughshod over them.

In following Jesus, we are called to declare war on the four horsemen of the apocalypse! The forces of darkness are for death, but the gospel is for life — wherever it is found — and against persecution, war, economic injustice and premature death.

THE FIFTH SEAL: *the suffering church*
(chapter 6, verses 9 to 11)

Jesus then opens the fifth seal and, under the altar, John sees the souls of those who had been slain because of the word of God and the testimony they had maintained. We are shown in this section that, as the horsemen ride across the world, there is suffering for the followers of Jesus. This is also what Jesus says in Matthew 24, verse 10:

> Then many will fall away, and they will betray one another and hate one another. And many false prophets will arise and lead many astray. And because of the increase of lawlessness, the love of most will grow cold. But the one who endures to the end will be saved. And this good news of the kingdom will be proclaimed throughout the world, as a testimony to all the nations; and then the end will come.

Those who proclaim this message are often martyred for their faith. Their souls are safe with God underneath the altar of God's temple (verse 9). But now they cry for vengeance (verse 20). This is not just a cry for personal vengeance, but for God to vindicate himself. They have been killed for what is *true*: now let God vindicate that testimony to himself!

As a final recognition of God's approval, they are given a white robe (verse 11) — a symbol of being clothed in Christ's righteousness — and told to wait a little longer. More martyrs are to be added to their number. And they have been. Rather than declining, the number of people actually dying for their faith has continued to grow throughout this century. The blood of the martyrs is, as Tertullian said, the seed of the church.

It is costly following Jesus. This teaching is not popular in large sections of the Western church. Some believe that, before the suffering of the church begins, Jesus is going to come back and take us all out of the world, followed by a period called 'the Great Tribulation'. To some, this view has come to be the touchstone of orthodoxy.

However, this is a relatively recent teaching in the history of the church. The biblical evidence for this point of view is extremely slight, but its results can be distressing. It can produce a complacency that says: 'Don't worry — we won't suffer. God will come and get us before this dreadful time occurs.'

I wonder how the following would have sounded to a Christian in one of Stalin's concentration camps? 'Brothers and Sisters, we are not going to face tribulation; Jesus is going to come and take us away.' Or, a bit closer to home, to Chinese believers during the cultural revolution: 'Brothers and Sisters, the saints will not go through the tribulation. People are being killed all around us in tens of thousands — but we are not going to face the tribulation!'

But John tells us quite clearly in the passage that, in spite of the suffering, the end has not yet come. Many have died and people are asking Jesus how long it will be before he comes back in justice. He gives them a white robe and tells them to wait a little longer.

Jesus said that one thing would determine the time of his return. It is not when some particular teacher's charts are complete. It is when the gospel of the kingdom has been preached in the whole world as a testimony to all nations (Matthew 24, verse 14). Christians are not called to be passive, and they are not called to sit back and say there is nothing we can do but wait for Jesus to come and put things right. They are called to be involved in the spread of the gospel throughout the earth.

American evangelist Billy Graham has said: 'The world's situation has reached a climactic point and it is going to continue to grow worse and reach some sort of climax which the Bible graphically describes in both the Old and New Testaments. But it is not enough for Christians to stand glibly by and applaud the impending Apocalypse. It is up to us to pray and work. As one individual, I can do very little. I only have one bucket of water to throw on the fire, but I am going to throw it with all my might, asking God to use it as he did the five loaves and two fishes.'[5]

THE SIXTH SEAL: *the end*
(chapter 6, verses 12 to 17)

John then watches as Jesus opens the sixth seal. There are powerful signs on the earth and in the heavens. This vision of cosmic upheaval presents a powerful picture of God's judgment on unrepentant humanity. Matthew 24 again gives us a similar picture: 'Immediately after the suffering of those days, the sun will be darkened and the moon will not give its light; the stars will fall from heaven and the powers of heaven will be shaken' (verse 29). Jesus here is quoting from the prophet Isaiah, chapter 13, verse 10. He then goes on in verses 30 and 31 to say:

> Then the sign of the Son of Man will appear in heaven, and then all the tribes of the earth will mourn, and they will see 'the Son of Man coming on the clouds of heaven' with power and great glory. And he will send out his angels with a loud trumpet call and they will gather his elect from the four winds, from one end of heaven to the other.

This is no secret, mysterious coming. Every passage in the New Testament that refers to Jesus' return describes a very noisy event. The angels are shouting, trumpets are being blown, and history as we know it is being wound up. The whole world, the whole universe, is going to see that Jesus Christ is Lord.

THE SEVENTH SEAL: *the 144,000*
(chapter 7, verses 1 to 8)

John has another vision. This time he sees four winds which will blow over the earth with destructive power, but which God is holding back until a certain event takes place.

This vision is parallel to the one John describes in chapter 6 but, in addition, it shows us something not shown in the vision of the four horsemen. Before the destruction is unleashed on the earth, before the four horsemen ride out or before the four winds blow — whichever vision we are looking at — God steps in and seals the servants of God: 'Do not damage the land or the sea or the trees, until we have marked the servants of God with a seal on their foreheads.'

We don't use seals so much today, but up to a hundred years ago they were still commonly used to indicate ownership. So this passage is saying that God has put his mark of ownership on his people. What is the seal of God? We are told that, when we come to Christ, we are *sealed* with the Holy Spirit. He is the mark of ownership that we belong to God (Ephesians 1, verse 13).

For those Christians who were being persecuted at the time John was writing, this could not have been a greater word of encouragement. They were in the midst of great persecution and John has reminded them that God had sealed them. They belonged to him.

Who are these people, the servants of God who are sealed? John heard the number of those who were sealed — 144 000. And they were from all the tribes of Israel. This passage has been a happy hunting ground for all manner of groups down through the history of the church!

This is serious stuff. If God is going to seal only 144 000, how do I know if I'm one of them? Some people say the 144 000 are the Jews, because it mentions all the various tribes — literally 144 000 Jews yet to live at some time in the future. The fact that some of the twelve tribes have seemingly disappeared without a trace does not appear to matter. The Jehovah's Witnesses say the 144 000 are themselves, invited by Jehovah God to go to heaven to rule with Jesus Christ — the rest of their movement will live on earth forever as subjects of his kingdom.[6]

So how do we understand it all? We need to be reminded that what we have here is a vision, and symbol is the language of vision. How much heartache would be saved if this obvious point was grasped. When it comes to the four horsemen, no-one thinks there is actually a man on a horse called War that will ride around the earth starting all the wars. It's obviously symbolic.

Likewise, the 144 000. This is a picture of comleteness.[7] In Jewish thought, twelve multiplied by twelve is the perfect square. Multiply it by 1000 —

it's a picture of vastness and completeness. There is a vast yet complete number of people who are called the servants of our God. God has sealed them and said to them that the world will experience deception, war, famine and death, but they can put their trust in him because they belong to him; he will not let them go. That is the message of the 144 000.

Who are these Jews? Are they really the Jehovah's Witnesses or the citizens of the modern nation state of Israel? What does the New Testament say? 'A person is not a Jew who is one outwardly... Rather, a person is a Jew who is one inwardly... it is spiritual and not literal' (Romans 2, verses 28 and 29). 'And if you belong to Christ, then you are Abraham's offspring, heirs according to the promise' (Galatians 3, verse 29). 'For it is we who are the circumcision, who worship in the Spirit of God and boast in Christ Jesus' (Philippians 3, verse 3). The true Jew according to the New Testament is the follower of Jesus.

Peter wrote to the early Christians and said, 'But you are a chosen race, a royal priesthood, a holy nation, God's own people' (I Peter 2, verse 9). What he did was to take Old Testament language that applied to Israel and apply it to the church. And then there is a fascinating verse at the very beginning of James: 'James, a servant of God and of the Lord Jesus Christ. To the twelve tribes in the Dispersion.'

By the time James came to write his letter, the early Christians were using this picture of themselves. They saw themselves as the twelve tribes who were scattered throughout the earth.

Who are the 144 000 Jews, then? They are a vast but complete number of people drawn from many peoples who are followers of Jesus. They are sealed by God, but they will go through difficulties. If Christians go to war, God does not promise that the bullets will bounce off their chests. If all around are suffering from famine, God does not promise them the stones will turn into bread. If there's destruction all around them, God has not said he will take them out of it. What he has promised Christians is that he will be with them. When they go through the fire, he says he will be there. When they pass through deep waters, he'll be there. John is saying to these people, 'Don't abandon hope, because God has put a seal on us that says we belong to him.'

In places where some Christians are taken away by secret police and others wait trembling for the knock on their door, this is a powerful message. God is not about to abandon them. He has put a seal on them and his seal is the Holy Spirit. It is a sign that God is not going to give up on them.

The vision of the final day
(chapter 7, verses 9 to 17)
Then the vision changes. We're back in heaven and

the suffering is all over. The trauma caused by the four horsemen and the four winds, the deception, war, famine and death is finished and the celebration of God's victory has begun. In the celebration are people out of every nation, tribe, people and language.

God has a dream for his people: they will be involved in the spread of the gospel throughout the whole world so that, as a result, people out of every nation and tribe and people and language will be there on that final day. The message of the book of Revelation is a call, not to passivity, but to mission.

In anticipation of the celebration in heaven, Christians are called to worship Christ and are called to live for the values of the kingdom. They are called to be involved in the world, spreading the gospel, living for justice and peace, and worshipping God. They are called to be a people who are anticipating the kingdom of heaven.

While the celebrating is going on, one of the elders comes to John and asks him, 'Who are these robed in white and where do they come from?' (verse 13). So John says to the elder, 'Sir, you are the one that knows,' and the elder says, 'These are they who have come out of the great ordeal; they have washed their robes and made them white in the blood of the Lamb' (verse 14). They have been through suffering and have been cleansed. The early Christians expected that suffering would be part of discipleship, so they looked forward to the end with great anticipation.

Then we come to the last part of this remarkable passage in verses 15 to 17. It has been said that, for many, this is the passage for which the book of Revelation exists.[8] Of all the peoples on earth, the followers of Jesus should be characterised by hope. Hope of the ultimate victory of God assured to us through the resurrection. And hope for our own lives when our time comes to go to be with the Lord, and to share in this worship and celebration.

When the great American evangelist D.L. Moody lay dying, it is reported that he sat up in bed and said: 'Earth recedes, heaven opens before me. If this is death, it is sweet! There is no valley here. God is calling me and I must go. . . This is my triumph; this is my coronation day! It is glorious!'[9]

Such is the anticipation we can have for our future life with God.

Discussion questions

Talking it through

1 Revelation chapters 4 to 7 is the first vision of John. It describes the 'coronation' of Jesus in heaven and his ascension to the right-hand of God. When, do you think, did this event take place?

2 What picture of Jesus Christ is given in chapter 5, verses 6 to 14? How is it different from the perspective we have in most other parts of the New Testament, especially those passages focussing on his suffering at the hands of unjust men?

3 Revelation 6, verses 1 to 8 describes the four horses of the Apocalypse. The third seal heralds a situation of economic deprivation — where people live, but only just. (Wheat was the rich man's fare; the coarser-grained barley was for the poor man. People could afford the bare minimum, but there was nothing left over for 'luxuries' like olive oil and wine.)

How does the third horse speak to us today? Do you expect your immediate economic circumstances to improve? Does this worry you/please you?

4 Revelation 6, verses 9 to 11 describes the destiny of those martyred for their faith. What clues are there in the expressions used that their death is not in vain and their spiritual welfare is secure? Do we need reminding of this truth today? Why?

5 How are these chapters a 'comfort'? Relate the following particularly to John's vision of the future. (in chapter 7, verses 15 to 17):
(a) A Christian black slave in the USA in the early nineteenth century
(b) A Christian Somali today looking starvation in the face
(c) A Christian abandoned by a spouse after thirty years' marriage

Widening our horizons

1 What is a vision? Compare it with each of the following:
 (a) Dreaming while sleeping
 (b) Extended day-dreaming
 (c) A trance.

 Can God use any of these to convey his ideas to us? What tests can be applied to determine whether messages we receive from each of these actually come from God? Is it belittling or glorifying to God to suggest he uses such means to convey his ideas?

2 Look at C.S. Lewis' ideas about praise (pages 28-29). How can each of the following enhance the worthwhileness of life:
 (a) Praise to the parents about their new-born baby?
 (b) Praise to a close friend/spouse about their kindness?
 (c) Praise to God about the beauty of a sunset?

3 How can the principles outlined in Revelation 6, verses 1 to 8 be applied to:
   (a) Government taxation policy?
   (b) International intervention in bloody civil wars?
   (c) First World attitudes to Third World debt?
   (d) Fellow citizens experiencing the effects of recession?
   What considerations make it difficult to apply these principles uncritically?

4 'A fulfilling life consists of an earthy awareness of the present and a vision for the future.' Is this true? Explain how you have been able to integrate the two in your life. Do you feel hopeful or pessimistic about the future?

5 Write a short poem or hymn praising God. This can be done as a special assigment to be read (or sung!) aloud when you next meet. Alternatively, you might like to paint a picture, make a wall-hanging or design a banner celebrating the goodness of God and his love for his creation.

2
The hope for humanity

REVELATION CHAPTER 8, VERSE 1 TO
CHAPTER 11, VERSE 18

THE PREVIOUS SERIES OF VISIONS reached its completion with the scenes of celebration in heaven. Now we are about to embark on the next series showing us, once again, the saga of life on earth between the first and second comings of Jesus.

The appearance of the seven angels
(chapter 8, verses 1 to 5)
After Jesus opened the seventh seal at the end of the previous visions, there was silence in heaven for about half an hour. In the writings of the Old Testament prophets, silence sometimes preceded the

judgments of God. Something momentous was about to happen and there was silence throughout heaven.

Seven angels appear on the scene and they are each given a trumpet. Before we are told what happens when the seven trumpets are sounded, John sees another angel: 'Another angel with a golden censor came and stood at the altar; he was given a great quantity of incense to offer, with the prayers of all the saints on the golden altar that is before the throne. And the smoke of the incense, with the prayers of the saints, rose before God from the hand of the angel' (verses 3 and 4).

What are all the saints praying about? In chapter 6, verse 10 we were told: 'They cried out with a loud voice, "Sovereign Lord, holy and true, how long will it be before you judge and avenge our blood on the inhabitants of the earth?"' The saints are praying for justice, not only in this verse, but also in chapter 8, verses 3 and 4.

Then follows the answer from God to these prayers. When the angel threw the fire-filled censer on the earth, 'there were peals of thunder, rumblings, flashes of lightning and an earthquake' (verse 5).

This seems a pretty tough answer! We see why when we get to the end of the chapter — God is longing that humanity will repent, come back to him and recognise that he is the creator.

This passage is a powerful incentive to prayer.

Many read the prophetic warnings of Revelation with a sense of hopeless pessimism. The trumpets will blow and there is nothing we can do about it. Yet, before the trumpets blow, there is silence in heaven. God can hear the cries of his people. His actions in justice are in direct response to these prayers.

The visions accompanying the angels' first six trumpet blasts (chapter 8, verse 6 to chapter 9, verse 21)

This vision of trumpets concerns the environment. 'They refer to woes that may be seen any day of the year in any part of the globe.'[1] 'The four [trumpets] are largely concerned with the forces of nature.'[2] There will be other visions later also concerning the environment, when seven bowls filled with the wrath of God will be poured out on the earth (chapter 15, verse 7 to chapter 16, verse 21). The trumpets are a warning from God that, when we see the earth being destroyed before our eyes, we are to see that he is calling humankind to repentance. We are to leave the foolishness of our ways and return to him.

Unfortunately, rather than seeing God at work through these judgments, many people have spent a great deal of time trying to identify them with one particular event occurring during their lifetime. This can miss the point of what the passage is saying to us.

It has been said that Christians don't have much

of a biblical understanding of the relationship between God and the earth — that the only verse we care about in this regard is the one that says God gave dominion to humankind over nature (Genesis 1, verses 28 to 30). We are told that Christians have interpreted this to mean we can do what we like — and so we have plundered the earth.

Lynn White, history professor at the University of California in Los Angeles, has been very critical of Western Christian attitudes to the earth.[3] In his view, the man who gave us an understanding of God's relationship to the earth was Francis of Assisi. Contrary to much current Western thinking, Francis believed that the earth was to be protected because it was God's creation and that the creatures of the earth, also God's creation, were to be protected, too. He preached to the animals and birds because they were God's creatures, calling on them to join in praising the Lord.

❑ *The first angel's trumpet blast*
'The first angel blew his trumpet, and there came hail and fire, mixed with blood, and they were hurled to the earth; and a third of the earth was burned up, and a third of the trees were burned up, and all green grass was burned up' (chapter 8, verse 7). Does this describe a specific event that will occur at some particular point between when Jesus first came to the earth and when he comes back again?

In 1745, there was an earthquake in Lisbon, Portugal, which wreaked great havoc. Some biblical scholars said this event was the fulfilment of Revelation 8.[4] Some people in our own day have said this passage is describing nuclear war. Others have said it is the bombing of Hiroshima and Nagasaki that is being described. It reads to me like napalm bombing in Vietnam!

If we ask which of these interpretations is right, the answer probably is: all of them. We are being shown what life will be like in the world between when Jesus first came and when he comes back again.

However, if we take a hold of one event, let's say the napalm bombing of Vietnam, and say that this passage is predicting the Americans would do this to the Vietnamese, we are left with a problem. What could this possibly have meant to the people for whom John wrote this revelation?

Any interpretation of this book must be one that would have made sense to the original readers and be a message of hope to sustain and encourage them. Rather than being a prediction of one particular event in the distant future, what we're being told is that this is what it will be like right through the period between Jesus' first and second coming. The human race has turned away from God, so these things will happen and continue to happen on the earth.

The fact that a third of the earth is destroyed in

these judgments is a warning. God is calling on people to repent. The purpose of a trumpet is to warn rather than to destroy.

❑ *The second angel's trumpet blast*
'The second angel blew his trumpet and something like a great mountain, burning with fire, was thrown into the sea. A third of the sea became blood, a third of the living creatures in the sea died and a third of the ships were destroyed' (chapter 8, verses 8 and 9). God's judgment continues now on the sea as well as the land.

We now know that the oceans are dying. Some years ago, Thor Heyerdahl journeyed across the Atlantic, about twenty years after he sailed the Kon-tiki raft across the Pacific. His purpose was to see whether the ancient Egyptians could have sailed to the Americas. He said that when he sailed across the Pacific it was a very beautiful experience but, crossing the Atlantic only twenty years later, he was surrounded by oil slicks, plastic containers, garbage and dead fish killed by human pollutants.[5]

Some of the biggest inland waterways in the world are now nearly dead, killed by humans, because we have not realised that this world is God's world, a gift to us to love and care for. Because we haven't recognised God as the creator, we have felt we could do whatever we wanted with the world. So John tells us that something like a huge mountain all ablaze has been thrown into the sea and we see the destruction before our very eyes.

❏ *The third angel's trumpet blast*
The third trumpet is blown. 'And a great star fell from heaven, blazing like a torch, and it fell on a third of the rivers and on the springs of water. The name of the star is Wormwood. A third of the waters became wormwood and many died from the water, because it was made bitter' (chapter 8, verses 10 and 11).

The foreign minister of Byelorussia, speaking at the United Nations in 1990, quoted this verse. He said that one fifth of the population of his republic had become innocent victims of the 1986 Chernobyl nuclear power plant disaster. Noting that a Slavic translation of Chernobyl can mean 'wormwood', he said, 'and many people died from the waters that had become bitter'.[6]

Chernobyl will not be the only fulfilment of this prophecy. But Chernobyl is typical of what is going to keep happening throughout this age. No one particular event fulfils these prophecies, but the general destruction of the earth that we are seeing is a fulfilment of this passage. Disaster will follow disaster and it is an expression of the judgment of God.

❏ *The fourth angel's trumpet blast*
'The fourth angel blew his trumpet and a third of

the sun was struck, and a third of the moon, and a third of the stars, so that a third of their light was darkened; a third of the day was kept from shining, and likewise the night' (chapter 8, verse 12).

At the end of the 1980s, we became aware of the plight of the rainforests of Brazil. When rainforests are burned, at midday the sky is black. Forests are being burned so people can grow crops and graze cattle. More and more land has to be cleared because the soil is so bad that crops can't be grown in any one place for long. Nor can cattle be grazed for long periods, so increasing amounts of land are needed. It is greatly feared that the whole of the earth's fragile climatic system could be permanently altered.

Why are the Brazilians burning their rainforests? Basically because they owe rich nations billions of dollars and growing crops for export is one attempt to pay the interest owing on these loans. So the cost of the Brazilians borrowing such large sums is being felt globally in the destruction of the environment. Here, we have an illustration of this fourth type of judgment.

In seeing illustrations, however, it is important to bear Wilcock's observation in mind: 'The supernatural events of the Bible are concerned not with "How?"; but with "Who?" and "Why?"'[7]

❑ *The fifth angel's trumpet blast*
Interpreting the fifth trumpet is a challenge! Tor-

mentors come out of the bottomless pit to destroy like plagues of locusts. This is the kind of passage that gives many popular end-times preachers a field day. How are we to understand it?

Fortunately, as is the case in many of the visions in Revelation, a clue is given in the text. We not only read of these fearsome locusts, but we read the name of their leader is Destroyer (verse 11). Bearing in mind that symbol is the language of vision, we can understand that what John saw were demonic hordes coming from the bottomless pit to torment people for 'five months'. The fact that the torment was for 'five months' probably means people are not tormented continually, but for a limited period. We think this is bad enough, but worse is to come!

❏ *The sixth angel's trumpet blast*
The sixth trumpet is blown. Two hundred million demons appear and they begin to wage war on humankind (chapter 9, verse 16). This is quite similar to the four horsemen of the apocalypse who, we were told, were given power over a fourth of the earth to kill by sword, famine, plague and by the wild beasts of the earth. In this vision, a third of the earth dies, the effect of these two hundred million demons.

The BBC made a documentary called 'The Fatal Attraction of Adolf Hitler', in which the commentator talked about Hitler's 'demonic vision'. World War II was one example of the fulfilment of what we have here. When sinfulness and rebellion against God gain the ascendancy, the results *are* diabolical.

Why doesn't God stop it? Why does he let people continue in their sin? Verses 20 and 21 tell us God is longing that people will repent. This passage is like the account of the plagues in Exodus. When the people were slaves in Egypt, God told Moses to go to Pharaoh and tell him to let the Israelites go. Moses did this, but Pharaoh 'hardened his heart' and said No. Moses told him that plagues would come. One plague followed another and each was worse than the one before, until finally the first-born of all the families in Egypt died. Then, and only then, did Pharaoh let the Israelites go (Exodus 5 to 12).

Is our situation so hopeless we can only sit in despair waiting for the end to come? Surely not! The vision begins with the people of God in prayer. Do we believe God acts in the world in response to prayer, or not? Prayer is an act of rebellion against the sinful status quo.

The Bible shows that God is allowing all this to happen in the world because of his longing that people will come to repentance. These disasters finally come because people will not repent — they will not turn away — from the worship of demons, from idolatry, murder, magic arts, sexual immorality and theft, and turn back to God (verses 20 and 21).

But what about calling people to repentance? A widespread Christian mindset is that there's nothing we can do to prevent these dreadful things happening.

We have already seen that there is another way to look at all this — the way the Old Testament prophets did. The story of Jonah is a well-known example. God told Jonah to go to the people of Nineveh and prophesy that the city would be overthrown in forty days' time. There was no suggestion the people would repent or that God would do anything other than wipe out the city of Nineveh.

With great reluctance, Jonah went to Nineveh and called on them to repent and turn back to God, which they did. But Jonah still went outside the town to wait for judgment to fall. Forty days later, there was no judgment and Jonah was really upset. He wanted to see these people burn.

The longing of God's heart is that the people who are destroying the earth because of greed will repent and come back to him, and see this world as a beautiful gift. These destructive events happen because we have chosen to go our own way and not God's. Christians are good at believing that God is redeemer, but sometimes not so good at believing that God is creator. Often our understanding of the spiritual world is tied up with what goes on inside us: 'I have been redeemed and I am going to heaven.' But the Bible gives us a much bigger view.

He calls us to love the world that he has made.

The prophets dared to believe that God would act in the world. At the end of this chapter, we find God grieving that the human race has not repented and returned to him. The book of Revelation is a warning and a call to involvement. God loves this world and is grieved at the greed, destruction and hatred being unleashed on it. This is God's big vision — and we can share it. We can have such a vision of the nature of God and the gospel, and we can share this vision with others.

Some of us are in positions where we can influence people whose lives are motivated by greed and who care nothing for the things that God cares for. This chapter is a solemn warning that, if we turn from God, we will continue to face the terrible judgments which we are facing today. But things don't have to be as they are. The people of God can make a difference.

The vision of the mighty angel and the little scroll (chapter 10, verses 1 to 11)

Six trumpets have already sounded but, before the final trumpet is blown, there is a pause. John sees a mighty angel coming down from heaven. He is vast, and he places one foot on the sea and one on the land. In his hand is a little scroll.

Something very important is about to happen and, as John is listening to this angel, he hears seven thunders speak. He starts to write down what he is about to hear, but a voice says to him: 'Seal up what the seven thunders have said and do not write it down' (verse 4).

The apostle Paul had an experience like that. He said he was taken to heaven and saw things that were so amazing he was not able to tell people what he had seen or what he had experienced (2 Corinthians 12, verses 2 to 4). I think this is reassuring, because it is telling us there are some things we don't know and that God doesn't want us to know. It means we have to approach the book of Revelation with humility.

Then the angel raises his hand to heaven and says: 'There will be no more delay' (verse 6). We think, this is it. Now we are going to hear the seventh trumpet blown and the end will come. Jesus Christ is going to return in power and majesty and they're going to start singing the 'Hallelujah Chorus'! But instead, something else happens.

This is a very frustrating book to read! Why does the end not come?

John is told to take the little scroll out of the hand of the mighty angel and eat it. As he puts it in his mouth, it is sweet but, as he swallows it, it turns bitter. Ezekiel had a similar experience (Ezekiel 3, verses 1 to 3).

There is nothing sweeter than the message of the gospel. Nothing is more beautiful than the message that Jesus loves us even when we are so hardened in our sin that we turn away from God. Yet it produces bitterness and hostility because it is a terrible threat. The early Christians experienced persecution because the invitation to follow Jesus was a threat, a powerful challenge to people's pride. This beautiful message can lead to a dreadful experience of bitterness and persecution.

God was saying to John that, while all these things would befall the earth, our mandate is to take the message, go into the world and preach it. In the midst of the destruction, we are to call on people to repent. This is God's will. He made the earth. He loves it. We are called to be involved in this world, so that the values of the kingdom might be seen and people might be brought out of darkness into the light that his gospel produces.

The measuring rod and the two witnesses (chapter 11, verses 1 to 14)

Now the vision changes again. John has been given a measuring rod, and he is told to measure the temple and count the worshippers. What is he talking about? He cannot be talking about the Temple in Jerusalem because, by this time, it had been destroyed.

In 1 Corinthians 3, verse 16, we read: 'Do you not know that you are God's temple and that God's Spirit dwells in you?'; 2 Corinthians 6, verse 16 says:

'For we are the temple of the living God'; and Ephesians 2, verse 21 says: 'In him the whole structure is joined together and grows into a holy temple in the Lord.' The temple of God in the symbolism of the New Testament is the people of God. So John is told to go and measure the temple and count the worshippers.

As we study this vision, we discover some parallels with previous visions. As the four horsemen of the apocalypse were riding out on the earth, there was a pause: 144 000 people appeared and they were counted and sealed. Here again the people of God are measured and counted; God is going to look after them.

This is the powerful message that runs right through Revelation. God has not promised escape from tribulation, persecution and distress. The *World Christian Encyclopedia* claimed that, in 1991, 284 000 people around the world would be martyred for their faith in Jesus Christ.[8]

God has never said he is going to snatch us out of trouble and distress. But he promises he is going to keep his hand on us and, we are told this will continue for a period of 42 months, or 1 260 days, or three-and-a-half years. That's rather precise! Why three-and-a-half years?

In 168 BC, Antiochus Epiphanes invaded Israel, and the Jews were put to the sword. The Temple was desecrated: a statue of the Greek god Zeus was erected, pigs were slaughtered on the altar of the Lord, and the Temple precincts were turned into a brothel. The Jews rose up against Antiochus Epiphanes and tens of thousands, possibly hundreds of thousands, were killed. Then the Jews, led by Judas Maccabeus, were successsful in repulsing Antiochus Epiphanes. The period that Antiochus occupied Jerusalem was three-and-a-half years, from 168 BC to 165 BC. So a period of three-and-a-half years would have been highly significant to Jews. They would have understood it as a symbol for a time of persecution.[9]

While this persecution is happening, two witnesses emerge and begin to preach with great power. The two witnesses are the key to understanding this passage. 'And I will grant my two witnesses authority to prophesy' (verse 3). 'They are the two olive trees and the two lampstands that stand before the Lord of the earth' (verse 4). And, in verse 6, we are told: 'They have authority to shut the sky. . . and they have authority over the waters to turn them into blood, and to strike the earth. . .'

The two men in the Old Testament who shut up the sky so it didn't rain and who turned the rivers into blood were Elijah and Moses. But here they are mentioned in a symbolic way — so what do they stand for? We are given a few more clues. They are called the olive trees and the lampstands. The olive tree was a symbol for Israel, and the lampstand is a symbol for the church (Revelation 1, verse 20).

Moses and Elijah appeared to Jesus on the Mount of Transfiguration as he was on his way to Jerusalem to die. They represented Israel, both the law and the prophets. They were a sign of the people of God. So, during this time of persecution, the people of God, symbolised by Moses and Elijah, are to go into the world and proclaim the message of God. The message is to be proclaimed with the power of signs and wonders.

While they are proclaiming this message in great power, the beast climbs out of the bottomless pit and wages war on the people of God. They are killed and lie dead in the streets of Sodom and Egypt (verses 7 and 8). This is a symbol, we are told, for Jerusalem. The picture is of the followers of Jesus sharing in the fate of their Lord.

Some think this is all in the future, and Moses and Elijah are two actual people who will appear at some future date. But Revelation is not a religious version of the prophecies of Nostradamus! It was a message of profound hope to the first century Christians. They had been fed to the lions, boiled in oil, covered in tar and set alight in Nero's garden so he would have light during his garden parties. At the end of the first century during the reign of Emperor Domitian, they were systematically hunted out as enemies of the state (being non-participants in the state religion). The beast from the bottomless pit was waging war on Moses and Elijah, the people of God, and they were dying in large numbers. To these people, seemingly forsaken by God, comes this powerful prophetic word that death is not the end. The church may die, but God will raise it from the dead.

At times, the church will die and the enemies of the gospel will gloat as the bodies of Moses and Elijah lie in the streets. They won't even give them a decent burial. They will rejoice that, at last, they are rid of these Christians, once and for all. This was the situation in the first century.

Some see that this vision is of something that will happen just prior to the second coming. But a reflection on the history of the people of God will reveal many parallels to the death and resurrection experience. Leon Morris says, 'History has often seen the church pressed to the very verge of extinction, but it has always seen it rise again from that verge of death.'[10]

Mao Tse Tung thought he had achieved the same result in China when, after the Revolution, the Chinese communists set about systematically exterminating the Christian church. After the last of the missionaries were driven out of China around 1950, the bamboo curtain descended and nobody knew what was going on behind it. Would the million, or maybe two million Christians, survive? Were they dependent on missionaries from the West? What would happen to the church that had been established in China? Nobody knew. During the terrible years of the Cultural Revolution, millions died while the nation was in the grip of madness. Then the curtain began to lift and a church of tens of millions of people was found. It had died, the enemies of the gospel had gloated, but God had raised it from the dead.

It is estimated that in Africa in AD 500 (before the growth of Islam), forty per cent of Africans were Christians. But, by the beginning of the nineteenth century, only one per cent of Africa was Christian. The bodies of Moses and Elijah lay in the streets. The church had died. By the beginning of this century, even after a hundred years of missionary endeavour, still only nine per cent of Africa was Christian.

But the resurrection is occurring and God is raising the body of Moses and Elijah from the dead. In 1989, it was estimated that forty-five per cent of people throughout the whole continent of Africa were professing Christians. And it is estimated that, by the end of this century, possibly fifty per cent of Africa will profess to be active followers of Jesus. Growth of almost unprecedented proportions is occurring in the church in Africa. The bodies of Moses and Elijah were slain and people said, 'The church is dead.' But God is raising it to new life.

What happens at the end? God takes Moses and Elijah to be with himself. The identification with Jesus' suffering, resurrection and ascension is now complete. They have been through tribulation, suffering and pain, and then God says: 'Come up here! And they went up to heaven in a cloud' (verse 12). The end has come. Jesus returns in power and majesty, and he calls his people to be with himself.

The vision accompanying the seventh trumpet blast (chapter 11, verses 15 to 18)

'Then the seventh angel blew his trumpet, and there were loud voices in heaven, saying: "The kingdom of the world has become the kingdom of our Lord and of his Messiah, and he will reign forever and ever"' (verse 15).

What a powerful message for the early Christians. They gathered for worship not knowing who would be there Sunday by Sunday. Then they receive this revelation from God that it is he who raises the dead — even though their brothers and sisters die and even though the church seems to die. God will raise the dead and Jesus finally will triumph. The kingdoms of the world will become the kingdom of our Lord and of his Christ and he will reign forever and ever! Not Nero. Not any other tyrant. The future belongs to Jesus!

74/The hope for humanity

Discussion questions

Talking it through

1 What do you feel is the *main* point of the visions in the book of Revelation?

2 How can these very specific visions be interpreted in such a way that they are meaningful to us as well as to Christians in the first century? Why is it right to see the visions as having this dual message?

3 What is there about God's nature that makes the concept of a judgment essential?

4 What are the various forms that the bitterness of the gospel might take today (chapter 10, verses 1 to 11)? Is Christianity an optimistic or pessimistic faith?

Widening our horizons

1 Bearing in mind God's eventual judgment, what do you believe your attitude should be to present injustice? To clarify your thinking, give your response to the following people:
  (a) Two brutal insurgency groups who victimise innocent children
  (b) A father who continues to abuse his teenage daughter sexually, but cannot be brought to account
  (c) A person who continues to damage your reputation by wrongful accusations to protect himself.

2 From what might people repent in each of the following cases of environmental degradation? (Please find answers that go *beyond* the pollution of the environment to its cause.)
  (a) The pollution of waterways by a chemical plant
  (b) A major polluting explosion in a nuclear reactor
  (c) The smog over our cities from factories and vehicle exhaust

(d) The global smog from the burning off of rainforests?

3 If 'progress' means growth of the church in the way it happens in Revelation 11, verses 1 to 14, why do you think there is little 'progress' in the Middle East and north Africa today? Why do you think there is so much 'progress' in the rest of Africa, Russia and eastern Europe today? Are there any important conclusions we can draw from this?

4 What potential do each of the following have in resolving all outstanding issues in the cosmos?
(a) The Christian hope of Revelation 11, verse 15
(b) The vision for the future of your favourite political party
(c) The vision for the future of some non-Christian religion — Islam, for instance.
(d) The vision of the future held by a dedicated environmentalist.

3
The church and the powers

REVELATION CHAPTER 11, VERSE 19 TO
CHAPTER 15, VERSE 4

❦

THE CHAPTER DIVISIONS IN REVELATION are not part of the original text of the Bible. They were added in the Middle Ages. There is a story that someone put them in while riding horseback from Madrid to Paris. Others have said it looks like it! So the chapter divisions are only approximations of where one theme ends and another one begins. This particular series of visions begins at chapter 11, verse 19, following the celebration of the victory of God that concluded the previous series of visions.

The woman and the dragon
(chapter 11, verse 19 to chapter 12, verse 6)

'Then God's temple in heaven was opened' (verse 19) is similar to the opening statement in some other scenes — for example, 'I looked and in heaven the temple was opened' (chapter 15, verse 5) and 'I saw heaven standing open' (chapter 19, verse 11).[1]

The sight of the ark of the covenent conveys the thought that we are seeing into the very presence of God himself. Thunder, earthquakes and similar phenomena often accompanied the actions of God in the Old Testament.

The vision of the woman and the dragon is about the most beautiful woman in the world: 'A great portent appeared in heaven: a woman clothed with the sun, with the moon under her feet, and on her head a crown of twelve stars' (chapter 12, verse 1). A woman couldn't look much more glorious than that!

Who is she? Over the years many people have looked at this vision and come up with various ideas. For many Roman Catholics, she has obviously been identified as the Virgin Mary. Mary Baker Eddy founded the Christian Science movement and I understand she rather modestly suggested that it might be herself! In the many commentaries on Revelation it is unusual to find people agreeing on much, but virtually everyone agrees the woman is the one from whom the Messiah was born, Israel. Israel is referred to in the Old Testament both as a wife and mother. 'In this symbolism we must discern Israel, the chosen people of God,' says Leon Morris.[2]

How do we make sense of this today? Some people suggest this amazing woman, Israel, is to be identified with the State of Israel that came into existence in 1948. I am not convinced of this. In the Old Testament, the name 'Israel' referred not just to a nation, but to the people of God. In the New Testament, references to 'Israel' speak of the followers of the Messiah, Jesus Christ.

Not only did the woman give birth to the Messiah, but she gave birth to some others. We are told in verse 17 that the dragon went off to make war against the rest of her offspring — those who obey God's commandments and hold to the testimony of Jesus. The woman's children are the followers of Jesus. And the woman is the mother of all who follow Jesus.

The Bible tells us God is our Father, but we have a mother, too — the church. Like a mother, the church is to provide warmth, security, love and affection and it is here we discover the tenderness and affection of God. For the early Christians living in a hostile world, this would have been a very meaningful picture.

Some today find it difficult to understand God as their Father, because they've had such bad experiences with their earthly father. When we start talking about God as a Father, all they can think of is a man who brutalised them. In the same way, some find it very difficult to think of the church as their mother, because they've had bad experiences of the church.

But that's not how God intended it to be. God intended the church to be a place of security, warmth and love. So here is this beautiful woman with crowns in her hair. She is the church of Jesus Christ, the people of God. There is continuity here between the Old and the New Testaments. When God called Abraham, a community of faith was brought into existence. Israel, the people of God, continued on through Old Testament times. The Israel of God today are those who follow Jesus, those who are the church, our mother.

She is about to give birth when another character appears on the scene. He is ugly, a contrast to her beauty. He is described in this way: 'A great red dragon, with seven heads and ten horns, and seven diadems on his heads' (verse 4). And the purpose of this monster is, quite simply, to devour the baby this mother is about to bring to birth.

Some people are really excited about the meaning of the seven heads and the ten horns, but remember, it is symbol. I imagine a seven-headed monster is a pretty difficult being to get rid of. The ten horns speak of power and the seven crowns indicate that he controls the kingdoms of the world. But he does not have total power, as only a third of the universe is affected by what he is doing. Only God has total power.

So this woman gives birth to the child. All we are told here about the life of Jesus is his birth and ascension. For the purposes of this story, we don't need to know anything else. He was born and returned in triumph to the Father, and the woman fled to the desert for three-and-a-half years. We saw in the last chapter how three-and-a-half years represents a time of persecution.

The conflict in heaven
(chapter 12, verses 7 to 9)

Now we look behind the scenes to see what is going on in heaven. For many of us, our picture of heaven is of people lying on clouds playing harps, but it says here a war is being fought in heaven, a conflict happening behind the scenes.

So we should understand 'heaven' as referring to the spiritual world, in the sense that Paul speaks of 'the spiritual forces of evil in the heavenly realms' (Ephesians 6, verse 12). It is not necessary to see this passage in Revelation as being in chronological sequence to the passage before it. That passage showed us symbolically the clash between the people of God and the devil. Now these next verses show us the spiritual conflict going on behind the scenes.

'The great dragon was thrown down, that ancient serpent, who is called the devil and Satan, the deceiver of the whole world' (verse 9). The devil is defeated and hurled out of heaven. When Jesus died on the cross, the devil thought he'd won, that goodness and truth had been defeated. But Jesus broke the power of death, rose from the grave in a great victory, and went back to heaven in triumph.

Jesus said during the course of his ministry: 'I watched Satan fall from heaven like a flash of lightning' (Luke 10, verse 18) and, as he prepared to go to the cross, he said: 'Now is the judgment of this world; now the ruler of this world will be driven out' (John 12, verse 31). So the shouting begins in heaven. The devil has been thrown out. 'Now have come the salvation and the power and the kingdom of our God and the authority of the Messiah' (verse 10). We wonder if this is the end.

Instead, we find to our horror that Satan has been hurled down to the *earth*! We wonder how it can be that Jesus has won this great victory over the devil and yet the powers of darkness are so obviously at work in the world. The most helpful illustration I have heard comes from German theologian Oscar Cullman, who saw a parallel to this in World War II:

> I may illustrate this idea by an example: *The decisive battle in a war may already have occurred in a relatively early stage of the war and yet the war*

still continues. Although the decisive effect of that battle is perhaps not recognised by all, it nevertheless already means victory. But the war must still be carried on for an undefined time, until Victory Day.

Precisely this is the situation of which the New Testament is conscious, as a result of the recognition of the new division of time; the revelation consists precisely in the fact of the proclamation that *that event on the cross, together with the resurrection which followed, was the already concluded decisive battle* [italics in original].[3]

On D-Day, 6 June 1944, the Allies invaded Normandy and established a beachhead. That day, the most decisive battle of World War II was fought and won and, from that point on, the outcome of the war was never in doubt. But it was nearly a year from that day before the Nazis were finally defeated. Some days it seemed the battle was going one way and sometimes another but, because of the victory on D-Day, the final victory on V-Day was assured.

Cullman says this is what it is like with Jesus. The resurrection was D-Day. The devil was defeated. V-Day, the final day of victory, is assured. But the fiercest fighting of World War II occurred after D-Day, not before. That is what it has been like since the resurrection and, as we see in Revelation, the conflict intensifies between the forces of light and of darkness.

Understanding the conflict
(chapter 12, verses 10 to 12)

The devil is cast down to earth with one supreme task. He is an accuser. His task is to accuse us, to make us hate life, to hate other people and ourselves. The early Christians knew what this meant. There were people in their day who hated them because they were a threat to society. There were secret police, informers and accusers and, on the basis of the accusations, some of the Christians would go to the lions.

It is like that for many of those who believe in Jesus around the world today. The battle ebbs and flows. The devil says to us, 'How can you be a follower of Jesus? Think of all the things you've done in the past! How can you say that you follow God?' But we know where these whispers come from.

How did the early Christians overcome the devil and his accusations? First, they overcame him through the blood of the Lamb. That's a reference to the cross. When we put our trust in Jesus Christ, God wipes the slate clean; he no longer accuses us. We are told: 'If we confess our sins, he who is faithful and just will forgive us our sins and cleanse us from all unrighteousness' (1 John 1, verse 9). If we hear these accusations — and many do — remember they are lies! When Jesus died on the cross, he bore our sin, cleansed us and forgave us.

That's the blood of the Lamb.

Second, they overcame him 'by the word of their testimony' (verse 11). They spoke about what Christ had done. There is power in doing that. It nails our colours to the mast.

Third, they overcame the devil because they were willing to die for their faith in Christ (verse 11). How can we overcome the devil by dying? Surely if we die, the devil has won a victory. Not so. The devil only gains a victory when someone falls away from faith in Christ. This issue would have been very real for these people. The person in the church in Pergamum, for example, who read out this letter would have known that some people listening might well die in the coming months.

I think this could be one of the reasons this book is such a mystery to us. Living and dying for the faith are not real issues for us any longer. Some people might offer abuse, but people don't usually want to kill those who have faith in Jesus. Maybe it will come. But it is a remarkable fact that, by being willing to die for Jesus, these people won a great victory over the power of Satan. William Barclay has said: 'The person who has remained faithful through suffering has proved superior to every seduction of Satan.'[4]

Jesus is calling people to be faithful and, if need be, to die. Do we want to follow a Jesus like that? This is not the Jesus of the Western church today, the one who will help me get lots of fun out of life and make things go better for me.

The Gospel calls us to lay down our lives for Christ. The result of hearing that message sustained the early Christians, and week by week their numbers grew. This is happening all over the world today where people are dying for their faith in Christ.

The conflict intensifies
(chapter 12, verses 13 to 17)

But the conflict is not confined to heaven: the devil has come to earth, he's filled with fury, his time is short and the battle is joined. In this final section, we find the battle raging and Satan persecuting the woman, who flees to the desert. This is a graphic picture which describes with vivid symbols the experience of the early Christians.

Jesus gave a warning to his disciples to flee to the hills when they saw the armies surrounding Jerusalem (Luke 21, verses 20 to 24). In AD 70, the armies did surround and finally crush Jerusalem. But before this happened, a prophet in the early Christian community in Jerusalem had a revelation from God that the time had arrived, that the Roman armies were ready to attack Jerusalem. So the Christians left the city and went into the desert, to a community named Pella, where they survived the dreadful destruction of Jerusalem — because they had believed the word of Jesus.[5]

This vision shows us this age will be marked by two things. The first is persecution from Satan, and the second is the special care of God in the face of this persecution. Is it only in the poorer nations of the earth, where the conflict with evil is stark in the way it was in the first century, that the gospel of Jesus Christ can triumph today? Or can God find the kind of Christians who can confront evil in the Western world, where the battle is more subtle?

The beast from the sea
(chapter 13, verses 1 to 10)

John now sees the dragon standing by the seashore and a beast coming out of the sea. It has seven heads and ten horns. This description of the beast is very similar, but slightly different to that of the dragon. The idea would be that the work carried out on earth by the beast is a manifestation of the power of the devil. This beast is given power to rule over the earth and to persecute the followers of Jesus.

Daniel had a vision similar to this one. He saw four beasts, one after the other. One looked like a lion, one like a bear, one like a leopard and the fourth was just monstrous (Daniel 7, verses 1 to 7). The vision that John sees is, in fact, all four beasts together and this gives us a clue to how it would have been understood by the early Christians.

To Daniel, the four monsters represented four successive kingdoms that were to rule the earth. The early Christians would not have had to guess who the beast in their day might be. It was obvious. Rome ruled the world and had, by this stage, become a beast. Rome was persecuting and killing the followers of Jesus.

The beast, however, is more than Rome. Rome was a particular manifestation in history of the power of the beast. Once Rome was gone from the stage of history, the power of the beast was expressed through other systems and tyrants. 'The sea-borne beast symbolises the persecuting power of Satan embodied in all the nations and governments of the world throughout all history,' says Hendriksen.[6]

However, the apostle Paul, when he wrote about the Roman Empire, seemed to be saying something quite different. He says: 'Let every person be subject to the governing authorities; for there is no authority except from God, and those authorities that exist have been instituted by God. Therefore whoever resists authority resists what God has appointed, and those who resist will incur judgment' (Romans 13, verses 1 and 2). Paul was describing the Roman State as the servant of God. Therefore the followers of Jesus must obey the State because it has been ordained by God to maintain peace and justice.

But when we come to Revelation 13, the same

Roman Empire is no longer seen as the servant of God. It is now seen as a beast. What had happened in the space of just a few decades? The Roman Empire had begun to take to itself the power that belongs only to God. Every human State needs some form of government or it cannot exist. It is given by God for society's good, so that it may reflect God's values of justice and peace. But, once a State begins to take to itself power that belongs only to God, it becomes a beast. The State has been instituted by God, but its powers are limited. Every politician needs to understand this: that the powers of the State are limited. Only God has supreme power.

But the Roman Emperor had declared that he was to be worshipped as a god. The State had become an instrument in the hands of Satan to persecute and put to death those who refused to confess that Caesar was Lord. Something good given by God had become an instrument of Satan, and this can happen to any human government. When any government takes upon itself the power that belongs to God, it becomes a manifestation of the power of the beast. The beast is under the control of the dragon, Satan, who hates what God has done and seeks to destroy it wherever he can.

In verse 3, we see that one of the heads of the beast seems to have suffered a death-blow, but its mortal wound had been healed. When the persecution was most fierce, perhaps the early Christians thought that if only the empire could be overthrown, the power of the beast would be ended. But when the empire was finally overthrown, the power of the beast did not end. It was simply manifested in different ways. What seems to be a fatal wound to the beast turns out not to be so. Sometimes through history it looks as if the beast is going to be destroyed, but horrifyingly it is not. When the beast that was the Roman Empire was overthrown, the beast itself was not killed — it rose again in different forms.

In the twentieth century, we have seen the manifestation of the power of the beast over and over again. There was Hitler, then Stalin, Mao Tse Tung, Idi Amin, Pol Pot, Saddam Hussein — and who knows who will be next? Millions have been killed through these particular manifestations of the beast.

What is the Christian response? Western society, rooted in Christian values, has recognised that the State has limited powers. But that is not the case in every part of the world. If we live in a country manifestly ruled by the beast, what should we do? We are told here what we are to do. We are to engage in non-violent resistance: 'Let anyone who has an ear listen: if you are to be taken captive, into captivity you go; if you kill with the sword, with the sword you must be killed. Here is a call for the endurance and faith of the saints' (verses 9 and 10).

Some Christians say we should do nothing. If we live in a society where the innocent are being massacred, we are to do nothing, it is said, because it is a political issue which is of no concern to us, because Christians are only to be concerned with people's spiritual lives.

But why, then, was this word given? We will only be taken into captivity if we resist the beast and his power. If we do nothing, the beast will leave us alone. But doing nothing is to give in to the power of the beast and this is why John brings this word. We are called to resist the power of the beast, but we are called to resist non-violently. John knew the people in the seven churches. People were dying for their faith in Christ because the Roman Empire had claimed power to itself that it had no right to take. And this is the word he gives to them — if you are to be taken captive, into captivity you go.

Jesus engaged in non-violent resistance. He knew those with power were out to get him, so he went to the Temple in full view of everybody, when the worshippers were going to make their offerings to the Lord. The rich were ripping off the poor with the Temple tax, and he took a whip in his hands, drove the animals out of the Temple, overturned the tables and said: 'My house shall be called a house of prayer; but you are making it a den of robbers' (Matthew 21, verse 13).

That's resistance against the power of the State. But it was non-violent resistance because, when he was brought before Pilate, he said: 'My kingdom is not from this world. If my kingdom were from this world, my followers would be fighting to keep me from being handed over to the Jews' (John 18, verse 36). Jesus submitted to the State and died. We are called to be his followers in this as in all else.

The beast from the earth
(chapter 13, verses 11 to 15)

We might think that would be enough for one vision, but there is more to come. Out of the earth comes a second beast. He looks like a lamb, but he speaks like a dragon, and he has the power to do signs and wonders.

This beast is the false prophet. He may look like Jesus and he may have the power to do signs and wonders, but he speaks like a dragon. The purpose of this false prophet is to encourage the devotion that rightly belongs to God to be given to the State, the first beast.

The early Christians would not have found this hard to understand. In Revelation 2, verse 13, we read of the church in Pergamum. John had written to them: 'I know where you are living, where Satan's throne is. Yet you are holding fast to my name, and you did not deny your faith in me even in the days of Antipas my witness, my faithful one, who was killed among you, where Satan lives.' Satan had his throne in Pergamum, a centre of Caesar worship, and resisting the powers meant death. So the early Christians knew that for them the function of the second beast, the Roman religious system, was to get people to give to the State the allegiance that rightfully belonged to God.

There is no problem as long as the State does not demand this allegiance, but who do Christians obey once there comes a conflict of loyalties? Do we obey the masters who run the country, or do we obey Jesus Christ? In many parts of the world there is conflict and, as we in the Western world move further away from our Christian roots, increasingly we will have conflict.

We have seen how the second beast operated in the Roman world. What about down through history? Martin Luther was quite clear about the second beast: it was the Catholic church and the Pope was the anti-Christ. And the Catholics were quite clear who the second beast was — it was State church Protestantism! When the Protestant churches broke with Rome, they formed national churches under the authority of the secular ruler. Today it may be a more nominal headship but, 400 years ago, the Protestant churches were hand-in-glove with the secular powers and the Catholic church said that the

Protestant churches were a manifestation of the power of the beast. But medieval Catholicism was also hand-in-glove with the secular powers.

The Anabaptists took the Reformers to task for not being radical enough in their desire to form churches like the New Testament church. Most of them were pacifists, refusing to serve in the army, claiming that the State should have no power over the church — Church and State should be separate. This was too much for the Catholics and the Protestants, and so they combined to kill tens of thousands of Anabaptists who saw in *both* the Catholic and Protestant churches manifestations of the power of the second beast.

What about this century? Where have we seen groups that looked like the real thing, but who urged people to give allegiance to the State instead of to God? What about the German Christians in Nazi Germany? When Hitler came to power, he spoke much about the Aryan master race. He thought the church should reflect these values which, he said, were given by God, and the church should therefore expel from its membership all who were not true Aryans. The majority of people in the churches in Germany meekly lined up behind Hitler.

But some didn't and the Confessing church came into existence. Their confession of faith declared that Jesus Christ alone was Lord and God. Their leaders were people like Karl Barth, Martin Niemoller and

Dietrich Bonhoeffer. Some ended up in concentration camps and some were exterminated. These leaders saw what was happening in the church in Germany as the power of the second beast.

The mark of the beast
(chapter 13, verses 16 to 18)
If we bear the mark of someone, it means we belong to that person. The task of the false prophet is to get people to bear the mark of the beast. 'It causes all, both small and great, both rich and poor, both free and slave, to be marked on the right hand or the forehead, so that no-one can buy or sell who does not have the mark — that is, the name of the beast or the number of its name' (verses 16 and 17).

By contrast, we can have God's mark. In chapter 7, verse 3, we read: 'Do not damage the earth or the sea or the trees, until we have marked the servants of our God with a seal on their foreheads.' So there are actually two marks we can get. We can bear the mark of Christ or we can bear the mark of the beast. The mark on people who have sold themselves to the beast and his values is the number 666.

I have read quite a number of commentators on this, and most of them explain this number differently! Many people try to identify 666 with a particular person, and this is where they differ. Some say it is the Pope, Luther, or even Hitler. An explanation for Hitler is reached by giving each letter of the alphabet a number: A equals 100, B equals 101, and so on. When we add up the letters h-i-t-l-e-r, it totals 666. How about Caesar Nero? In the Hebrew alphabet, numbers are represented by letters. If we take the title 'Caesar Nero' in Hebrew, it actually adds up to 666. The only problem is that Nero was already dead and John didn't write in Hebrew!

This kind of theorising misses the point. Repeatedly through this book, we have seen that symbol is the language of vision. We have already seen that the beast is not a particular individual. It is the power of the State demanding allegiance that belongs only to God. The mark of the beast speaks of the control of the State over the lives of individuals. John now invites us to use our wisdom to calculate the human symbol or number for the beast. The answer is 666.

John gives numbers specific meaning throughout Revelation. Three-and-a-half years is the number for the period between the first and second comings of Jesus. It has symbolic significance. Similarly, 144 000 is the number for the people of God. In a similar way, 666 is the number for the beast. If the way John uses numbers could only be grasped, thousands of hours of vain speculation about the identity of 666 could be avoided.

Michael Wilcock helpfully points out that often 666 is seen as one more clue in the puzzle to work out the identity of the beast. It is more than a clue; it is the solution to the puzzle.[7] Why six? It cannot be seven, as that is a symbol for the Holy Spirit (chapter 4, verse 5). Neither can it be eight, for that is greater than 7. But six falls short of seven. Furthermore, the recurring six is appropriate because that is the nature of evil: it is always there; you can't get rid of it. The number 666, therefore, is the human symbol representing the power of the beast to control our lives.

Revelation was written to people who were suffering under a tyrant. But let us not think that this is a message only for the Christians who live in China, North Korea, Iraq or some other country with a totalitarian regime. This is a very powerful word to us in the West. We produce religious systems that cause people to give their allegiance to the false values of our society and to think that materialism, greed and a promiscuous lifestyle are somehow approved by God. At the end of the day, all of us are going to stand before God and he's going to look to see which mark we are bearing. It could be 666 — demonstrating we have given our lives to the false powers of this world — or it could be the mark of the cross.

The Lamb and the 144 000 (chapter 14, verses 1 to 5)

We are coming to the end of the third series of

visions which began with the woman and the dragon, and the conflict that rages eternally between these two.

Now the scene changes and we see Jesus standing on Mount Zion surrounded by his followers. When we first read this passage, we can easily imagine all this is happening in heaven. However, the early Christians understood that when they belonged to Jesus, they were already standing with him on Mount Zion! 'It is quite in accord with scripture to speak of the entire church, living and dead, as being with God on Mount Zion which, though not an earthly location, is nevertheless a present spiritual reality,' says Wilcock.[8]

In Hebrews 12, verses 22 and 23, we read: 'But you have come to Mount Zion and to the city of the living God, the heavenly Jerusalem, and to innumerable angels in festal gathering, and to the assembly of the firstborn who are enrolled in heaven, and to God the judge of all, and to the spirits of the righteous made perfect.' The apostle Paul thought like this, too. In Ephesians 2, verse 6, he said: 'And [God] raised us up with him and seated us with him in the heavenly places in Christ Jesus.' Jesus reigns now and we share in this new resurrection life that he has given to us.

Look at the people who are gathered around Jesus. It is a bit disturbing because we find that it is not simply those who are not sexually promiscuous, but those who are *blameless*! We may wonder what hope there is for us, if the only people who can be with Jesus are those who are blameless.

But go back to the Hebrews passage again. Chapter 12, verses 23 and 24 says: 'You have come to God the judge of all, and to the spirits of the righteous made perfect, and to Jesus the mediator of a new covenant, and to the sprinkled blood that speaks a better word than the blood of Abel.' When it talks about the people who are perfect and blameless, it does so in the context of the new covenant. Before he was crucified, Jesus took the bread and the cup and said: 'For this is my blood of the covenant, which is poured out for many for the forgiveness of sins' (Matthew 26, verse 28).

The death of Jesus on the cross means that, when God looks on those who have committed their lives to him, he is blind to their past. There is a real sense in which he doesn't see that past because he has forgiven them through the cross. This is the most powerful and liberating message ever heard by the ears of any human being — but often we don't believe it! Jesus is standing on Mount Zion surrounded by all his people, saying, 'You're mine. You may not feel perfect and you may not feel blameless, but I am no longer blaming you for what has happened, for I have forgiven you.' In the midst of all the conflict being unleashed on humanity, we need Christian people who understand the reality of the forgiveness of God, who can stand secure in the love of God, and who will not be ripped apart by the storms of life.

This incident is another example of a theme that runs through the book of Revelation. Right throughout the age between Jesus' first and second coming, while there will be wars and famine, false prophets and systems that seek to control the minds of men and women, Jesus will be with us through it all! The two beasts have come out of the bottomless pit, but Jesus has his arms around his people and he has put his name and his Father's name on all those who belong to him. This is the message of the book of Revelation. As the church goes through suffering and faces death, Jesus will be with us and he will not abandon us.

Over the last 150 years, there has grown another school of thought on the book of Revelation. It is believed that, before the suffering begins, Jesus will return and take his followers out of the world, in what is called a 'secret rapture.' This view has become very widespread.

Revelation itself doesn't mention a secret rapture, although chapter 4, verse 1 is used to support this point of view: 'After this I looked, and there in heaven a door stood open! And the first voice, which I had heard speaking to me like a trumpet said, "Come up here and I will show you what must take place after this."' We are told that the words 'come up here' mean the whole church is caught up into heaven. At that point, the church disappears and the whole saga of Revelation happens![9]

But the straightforward meaning of Revelation 4, verse 1 is that it is an invitation to John to receive the revelations which make up this book. This teaching that Christians are not going to suffer through the tribulation is a convenient doctrine to believe. It gives people a great sense of security to think that, before the beast emerges, we are all going to be taken away. This teaching can only be believed in the Western world. I wonder how it is received by the brothers and sisters in China or Iran, or other places where people today suffer for their faith in Jesus Christ?

The three angels
(chapter 14, verses 6 to 13)

Verses 6 and 7 state: 'Then I saw another angel flying in midheaven, with an eternal gospel to proclaim to those who live on the earth — to every nation and tribe and language and people. He said in a loud voice, "Fear God and give him glory, for the hour of his judgment has come; and worship him who made heaven and earth, the sea and the springs of water."'

Some have seen this event as referring to a special end time angelic visitation. Others more correctly have seen it as a picture of the calling on the people of God to proclaim the gospel. 'It need not be doubted,' says Beasley-Murray, 'that John intended the loud voice of the angel to represent the tongues of Christ's witnesses in the time of tribulation.'[10]

This is what the people of God are called to be doing while this great cosmic conflict is enacted. It is not enough to be huddled with Jesus around Mount Zion seeking his solace. We are to be on the offensive, proclaiming the gospel throughout the earth, through every nation, tribe, language and people. But why an angel, when it is obviously people who do this? I would imagine it is because the work of spreading the gospel is never simply a human activity. It is, in fact, the work of God. Both human and divine dimensions are at work in it.

This call echoes what Jesus told his disciples. He gave one sign by which we could measure when the end would come — and it wasn't the number of nations in the European Community! 'And this good news of the kingdom will be proclaimed throughout the world, as a testimony to all the nations; and then the end will come' (Matthew 24, verse 14). He said that, not so we could draw up charts and speculate how everything will happen, but because we have a task to do — to take the message of Jesus to every nation, tribe, language and people. That's our response to the beast!

'Then another angel, a second, followed, saying, "Fallen, fallen is Babylon the great! She has made all nations drink of the wine of the wrath of her fornication'" (verse 8). We meet Babylon again in a few chapters. It is a symbol for the unjust systems of the world that oppress the weak and the powerless.

In the Bible, the call to proclaim both the 'eternal gospel' and the justice of God go together, but in the church we tend to separate them. We have a message to proclaim, that God is just. When he sees the poor being exploited and the voice of the powerless being stilled, his heart is grieved.

As if this is not enough, it is underlined that we are to warn individuals of the reality of the judgment of God. But if we choose to give our lives to the systems of this world that oppress the powerless, we had better beware because God loves justice. Those who choose to go the way of the beast and have his mark on them will, one day, stand before God to face his judgment.

The harvest of the earth
(chapter 14, verses 14 to 20)

The end has come. There comes a point when the gospel has been proclaimed to every language, people, nation and tongue, and some will not hear because they have hardened their hearts.

Two harvests are pictured here. The first is of wheat where Jesus gathers those who belong to him. For there to be a harvest, there has to be a sowing, and our calling is not so much to speculate on the date of the harvest as to give our energies to sowing the seed. Even Jesus has to be told when the moment of the harvest is to take place. The angel comes out of the temple and calls to him, 'The time has come!' In the Gospels, Jesus said he didn't know the time of the end. Only the Father knows (Matthew 24, verse 36). And this picture is quite consistent. Jesus is there as the Son of Man with a crown of gold on his head and a sharp sickle in his hand. He's ready, and waiting to be told the time.

It made me more than a little uncomfortable when some asserted with much confidence that 'Jesus is coming back in 1988!' Wrong again! When will they learn? Even *Jesus* doesn't know. We are not to give ourselves to endless speculations. Our task is to sow the seed.

Then comes the second harvest. It is of grapes — a picture of judgment. In fact, it is a dreadful picture of a bloodbath flowing for 300 kilometres, the length of Palestine. The whole land is swamped with a great sea of blood as high as a horse's bridle.

One passionate cry in the hearts of the early Christians was a cry for justice. We who live today often don't appreciate this because it's relatively easy for us to be Christians. They were being put to death by crucifixion, by being boiled in oil, by being fed to the lions and by being covered in pitch and set alight.

The cry on their lips, as surely as is the cry on the lips of our brothers and sisters living under repressive regimes today, is: 'How long, Sovereign Lord, before we will see your justice on the earth?' This was a powerful word to the early church. Just wait, because one day the tyrants will be overthrown and the world will see that love will win in the end.

The song of deliverance
(chapter 15, verses 1 to 4)

We are coming at last to the end of this long series of visions. John has a brief glimpse of the next vision in verse 1.

Then in verse 2 we proceed to the kind of celebration in heaven that characterises the end of each series of visions. The fact that the series ends in the middle of a chapter illustrates the fact that the present chapter divisions do not always follow the subject matter of the text. John saw 'what appeared to be a sea of glass mixed with fire, and those who had conquered the beast and its image and the number of its name standing beside the sea of glass with harps of God in their hands. And they sing the song of Moses, the servant of God, and the song of the Lamb' (verses 1 to 3).

Why the song of Moses? Because it was a song of deliverance. When the people of Israel were slaves in Egypt, God took them out of slavery and brought them through the Red Sea. At that point, they sang the song of Moses — 'I will sing to the Lord, fcr he has triumphed gloriously, horse and rider he has thrown into the sea' (Exodus 15, verse 1). It's a song of triumph and victory, and this song of deliverance is being sung in heaven because the Lord has won the greatest victory of all. The grave is empty. The victory has been won!

Discussion questions

Talking it through

1 What picture of the church do we have in Revelation 12, verses 1 and 2? Is this your experience of church?

2 How would the outline of the conflict in heaven in chapter 12, verses 7 to 9 have been on encouragement to the Christian church in the late first century? How can it be an encouragement to us?

3 Using the commentary on chapter 13, verses 1 to 10 as a guide, what action should we take if:
   (a) we live in a State where ethnic minorities are brutally attacked by a repressive military dictatorship?
   (b) we live in a State that outlaws the practice of Christianity?
   (c) we are imprisoned for our faith?

4 Do you see this section of Revelation as first and foremost depressing or helpful? Why do you think this way?

5 It is sometimes said that the primary task of the church is preaching Jesus' death and resurrection, not fixing up the world. What is there in this passage that suggests the two responsibilities cannot be separated?

Widening our horizons

1 How can having an earthly father like each of the following affect our attitude to God as Father:
 (a) a father whose main interest was TV, football?
 (b) a father who physically abused your mother?
 (c) a father who acted purely on the whim of the moment?

How can such a cycle be broken in our relationship with God?

2 As there is no overt persecution against Christianity in the West today, what sort of 'soldiering' is required in the face of each of the following:
 (a) the pursuit of purely materialistic goals?
 (b) the pursuit of the perfect body?
 (c) the pursuit of instant gratification?
 (d) the avoidance of suffering and death?

Indicate *one* way in which your writing of Revelation would have a different emphasis if you were writing it for Western society today?

110/The church and the powers

3 Perhaps the precise point at which Caesar became 'the beast' was when he set himself up as a god. Attempt to hazard a guess at a precise action taken by each of the following that could justify the label 'beast' being applied to them:
  (a) Adolf Hitler?
  (b) Joseph Stalin?
  (c) Idi Amin?
  (d) Pol Pot?

What did the action indicate about their view of themselves? What can we learn from this about ourselves?

4 What role can a church play in coping with the following types of injustice:
  (a) a government that discriminates against the poor in favour of the rich?
  (b) a local industry that damages the environment to the detriment of the local people?
  (c) a church leadership that covers up sexual abuse in its midst because it believes it is bad for its reputation if it becomes public?

4
The road to Armageddon

REVELATION CHAPTER 15, VERSE 5 TO
CHAPTER 16, VERSE 21

'AFTER THIS I LOOKED' in verse 5 marks the beginning of another series of visions. We have lived through a long series, starting with the conflict between the woman and the dragon, moving through the demand of the beast for our allegiance and ending with the harvest of the earth. Now we start another series.

This is by far the shortest of the seven series of visions. But, like several of the longer series, it contains seven events. We have previously met seven seals and seven trumpets. Now in these visions we meet seven angels with seven bowls.

This is what gives us the clue that we are dealing here with a whole series of visions, even though the section is so brief.

This chapter is almost a duplicate of Revelation 8, except that everything has intensified. In chapter 8, a third of the earth is devastated, but now the temperature has increased considerably. Not only is this one of the shortest visions; it's a very frightening one. We see what happens as God's wrath begins to be poured out on the earth.

Right through the book of Revelation, God calls us to repentance. Through war, famine, starvation, disease and the destruction of the environment, we find that God is calling out to men and women to leave the folly of their ways and repent. However, we now see that, in spite of all that is happening, people harden their hearts and refuse to repent. The message of this chapter is that, while God speaks to us through the things that happen between Jesus' first and second coming, there comes a point when the powerful of the earth will not listen. When that point is reached, the judgment of God begins to fall.

A remarkable parallel with this vision is found in the events of the Exodus. The reference to Moses in Revelation 15, verses 3 and 4 gives us the clue to understanding this passage. The people of Israel were slaves in the land of Egypt when Moses had a message from God to Pharaoh to 'let my people go' (Exodus 5, verse 1). But Pharaoh refused to listen to the voice of God and, as a result, plagues fell on the land. The plagues in Egypt parallel these plagues in Revelation.

And here we have echoes of the Exodus. On that occasion, God spoke — he sent a messenger to a very powerful man who held people under the yoke of oppression, and told him to release them. Pharaoh did not listen and the judgments of God began to fall. It affected the rivers and the sea, and people broke out in boils (Exodus 9, verse 8). But it was only a preview — like going to the movies when they show extracts from a coming film.

The first bowl
(chapter 16, verse 2)
In obedience to the instruction in Revelation 16, verse 1, the first angel in verse 2 'went and poured his bowl on the earth, and a foul and painful sore came on those who had the mark of the beast and who worshipped its image.' The Bible makes it very clear that we will suffer if we choose to violate God's principles for life. We were not made to live in hostility to God and, when we do, we suffer. Now the suffering becomes quite intense.

The second bowl
(chapter 16, verse 3)
Then the second bowl is poured out on the sea and the seas die. In the earlier warning in Revelation 8,

the seas partially die, but here the seas die totally. We might think that is impossible. But in the last two decades, some of the great inland waterways of the world have come to the point of being virtually dead, killed by pollution. We have the chilling prospect in the twentieth century of actually being able to accomplish some of the horrifying things that are mentioned here.

This raises the question of whether it is appropriate to look for signs of God's judgment in the events of history, or whether the bowls represent purely supernatural events at the end of time. But must we choose between these two alternatives? We see repeatedly with the Old Testament prophets that they could see the hand of God in events that others saw as only random happenings. In addition, they spoke of the 'Day of the Lord', when God would decisively enter human history.[1]

The third and fourth bowls (chapter 16, verses 4 to 9)

When the third bowl is poured out, the rivers turn to blood (verse 4). Here is another parallel with the book of Exodus. The angel passes comment in verses 5 to 7 that this is a reflection of the justice of God, because of human unrighteousness.

In verses 8 and 9, the fourth angel 'poured his bowl on the sun, and it was allowed to scorch them with fire'. This becomes more possible by the day with the removal of the ozone layer. 'They were scorched by the fierce heat, but they cursed the name of God.' As all this happens, God wants people to see the folly of their ways and turn back to him, realising that this earth is the creation of God. But instead of doing that, people curse the name of God and harden their hearts, just as Pharaoh did.

The fifth bowl
(chapter 16, verses 10 and 11)
What happens next? It gets worse. In verses 10 and 11, the fifth angel 'poured his bowl on the throne of the beast and its kingdom was plunged into darkness; people gnawed their tongues in agony and cursed the God of heaven because of their pains and sores, and they did not repent of their deeds.' The throne of the beast is the master stroke of Satan for the control of the earth.

As we saw in Revelation 13, the beast is any nation state that sets itself up and demands of its people an allegiance that belongs only to God. Down through history, the power of the beast has been shown in many different guises. Often when the end has come for a particular tyrant, it has been accompanied by scenes very similar to those in this passage. Some of the appalling events that marked the end of Nazi Germany would be one example. Still, the tyrants would not repent! Instead, they chose suicide or escape.

The sixth bowl
(chapter 16, verses 12 to 16)

In verse 12, the sixth angel 'poured his bowl on the great river Euphrates and its water was dried up in order to prepare the way for the kings from the east.' The Euphrates was the eastern border of the Roman Empire. Outside the empire lived the barbarians. So people come from all over the earth and gather together at a place that, in Hebrew, is called Armageddon. The word Armageddon means 'plain of Megiddo' — south-east of Haifa in modern Israel.

Michael Wilcock has an interesting description of the events that follow. 'Having seen his perversion of human society confounded, Satan says, "If I can no longer pervert, I will destroy," and he and the beast and the false prophet inspire the kings of the earth. . . to a frenzy of mutual slaughter.'[2] In a macabre way, the purposes of God and Satan come together. The devil thinks he is bringing about the destruction of humanity, but in fact it is the justice of God being exacted. It had happened once before. When the devil saw Jesus the Son of God here on earth, he sought to destroy him. At the cross he thought he had won, but Jesus in his death fulfilled the just purposes of God.

I believe the use of Armageddon here is symbolic. Other important place names in Revelation, such as Egypt and Babylon, are also symbolic. Why should Armageddon be chosen as the symbol? It was at the crossroads of the ancient world, since the road that went from Arabia to Europe passed across the plain of Megiddo, as did the road from Africa through Israel up to Asia. So the two main trade routes of the ancient world came together there and it was the scene of some of the most significant battles in human history, not just in biblical times.

It was at Armageddon that Gideon defeated the Midianites. When Sennacherib and his army of 185 000 invaded Israel and took Jerusalem, they were smitten overnight with the plague and died on the plain of Megiddo. There the Maccabees overthrew the Greek conquerors and brought liberty to Israel. Apparently Napoleon said that he thought it the ideal battleground for all the armies of the world — and proceeded to be defeated there! It is understandable why Armageddon was chosen — it is a very obvious symbol for war. Here it becomes the symbol for the final conflict between the powers of darkness, and Jesus Christ.

In the midst of this awful prediction, Jesus says: 'See, I am coming like a thief! Blessed is the one who stays awake.' And he adds a very homely illustration: remain dressed (verse 15). Be prepared. So right before this final cataclysm, this final act of judgment, we are reminded that Jesus is coming back. When the final showdown occurs between the powers of light and darkness, the reminder will be needed.

The seventh bowl
(chapter 16, verses 17 to 20)

Verse 17 shows how the seventh angel 'poured his bowl into the air, and a loud voice came out of the temple, from the throne, saying, It is done!' The earth is ripped asunder. After the San Francisco earthquake in 1989, much was written about our current understanding of why earthquakes occur. There are many plates that move against each other on the earth's surface and pressure builds up until finally they move. It is not possible to predict earthquakes accurately and no-one knows how strong each one will be. But here we have a picture that seems to describe a simultaneous movement of these plates on the face of the earth's surface. A quake of monumental proportions shakes the earth and civilisation, as we know it, comes to an end.

God takes seriously the needs of the poor, the oppressed and the weak. He looks on the powerful who oppress and enslave them and says that one day his justice will be revealed to the earth. This is the only one of the series of visions that does not end with scenes of the final triumph in heaven. Instead, there are scenes of God's final judgment on earth.

The awful warning of the Bible is that one day all of us have to stand before God, who will ask us what we have done with our lives. He will want to know whether we have responded to him in obedience. He will remind us that we knew him, we knew of his love, and we knew of his concern for the earth. Revelation is a call to mission, as is the whole of the Bible. The message is that we are not to be filled with terror and fear, but we are to respond to God's trumpet-call and proclaim that Jesus Christ, the creator of the universe, is coming back.

Discussion questions

Talking it through

1 'Wrath' is defined by the Macquarie Dictionary in this way:
(a) strong, stern, or fierce anger; deeply resentful indignation
(b) vengeance or punishment, as the consequence of anger.

To what extent does this definition suit the events described in this chapter? Is wrath appropriate for God?

2 'God has created a cosmos in which we have a great deal of power and, paradoxically, in which we have very little.' How does this passage in chapters 15 and 16 show that *both* those views are true? How does such knowledge make you feel? How does it affect your outlook?

3 What part does the Exodus story play in Revelation 16?

4 Using this passage and any other parts of the Bible you are aware of, what does the Bible teach about what will happen at the end of time as we know it?

Widening our horizons

1 'It is often difficult for us to see where God's judgment is being applied, but it is not so difficult for us to see what judgment from God we bring upon ourselves when the natural order of God's creation is transgressed.'

Do you think this is true in each of the following cases (be critical; if you are in a group, appoint a Devil's Advocate):
(a) sexually transmitted diseases?
(b) theft by the poor?
(c) the meltdown of nuclear reactors?
(d) the degradation of the rural landscape?

2 Where does the responsibility for evil lie: with the devil, with us or with God? Use the following events as examples of the way you feel this responsibility works:
(a) The slaughter of innocent people at the end of the Nazi era in Germany
(b) The death of Jesus
(c) The elimination of 'undesirable elements' in the Stalinist Soviet Union.

3 How do you account for the great curiosity there is about how the end of time as we know it will turn out? Why do you think people are so easily duped by those who peddle 'uncertain certainties'?

5
The system that seduces the world

REVELATION CHAPTER 17, VERSE 1 TO
CHAPTER 19, VERSE 10

REVELATION IS A 'TALE OF TWO CITIES'. Jerusalem and Babylon — the bride and the whore. We have already briefly met Jerusalem the bride, but now we meet the second woman, Babylon the whore.

The woman on the beast
(chapter 17, verses 1 to 18)
Babylon was used symbolically by the Old Testament prophets, because it was the place where the people of God were taken captive. The depth of feeling is apparent in this passage: 'By the rivers of Babylon — there we sat down and there we wept

when we remembered Zion. On the willows there we hung our harps. For there, our captors asked us for songs and our tormentors asked for mirth, saying, "Sing us one of the songs of Zion!" How could we sing the Lord's song in a foreign land?' (Psalm 137, verses 1 to 4).

It was an alien place and they were surrounded by things that contradicted the values of the kingdom of God. From that point on, Babylon became a symbol of any system that opposed the people of God.

The early Christians to whom John wrote did not need any explanation about what it meant. It was obvious: for them Babylon meant Rome, the city that controlled their lives, that marched off their brothers and sisters to the equivalent of the firing squad and the gas chamber. Rome was the economic and military system that ruled the world.

But Babylon is more than simply Rome because, when Rome was overthrown, that wasn't the end of unjust systems that exploit the peoples of the earth. One characteristic of Babylon and the beast is that they keep reappearing in different guises through history. Wherever there is a denial of human freedom, whenever there is persecution and injustice and oppression, there we find the beast. Wherever there is economic exploitation and trampling on the poor, there we find Babylon.

❏ Who is Babylon the prostitute?

While preparing this chapter, I heard a talk-back show on a Christian radio station. The topic was the second coming and the program guest asked callers to ring in and give their opinion as to who they thought Babylon the prostitute might be.

. Many people rang in to say the whore of Babylon is obviously the Catholic church. This was a view held by many Protestants at the time of the Reformation because of the persecution they received. (They somehow reconciled this with their persecution of Catholics and Anabaptists!) Such a view is supported by American Christian, Tim la Haye, who takes eight pages to try and prove that the whore of Babylon is the Catholic church.[1]

There is a real problem trying to identify Babylon with any Christian movement gone wrong. Babylon is always the 'harlot', never the 'adulteress'. She never was the wife of the Lamb. So in terms of the symbolism of Revelation, the wrong identification is being made.

But I believe such a view of the Catholic church, whether or not it was ever true, is not valid today. It is no more valid than saying the modern nation state of Italy is a manifestation of the power of the beast, ancient Rome. However, if we had asked that question about Italy in the 1930s and early 1940s when it was ruled by Mussolini, it can be argued that the answer would have been

Yes. It was a Fascist state built on principles of injustice.

Before we decide about the status of a particular movement, we have to look at the signs that are given in Revelation. What are the signs of the beast? What does the prostitute do?

❏ *What are the signs of the beast?*
We find Babylon the whore sitting on a beast. Verse 3 says, 'I saw a woman sitting on a scarlet beast that was full of blasphemous names, and it had seven heads and ten horns.' We met the beast in Revelation 13. The beast is the power of any state that demands of its citizens the allegiance that belongs only to God. In verse 9, there is a reference to 'the seven heads [who] are seven mountains on which the woman is seated'. It is generally assumed that this refers to Rome because Rome had seven hills. This does not exhaust its meaning, as seven in the book of Revelation is also used symbolically and we are told that the seven hills are seven kings. One thing we know for sure is that the power of the beast worked through the Roman Empire for the persecution of those who loved Jesus and who followed him.

In verse 8, we read something else about the beast. People who don't believe in Jesus are astonished at him: 'And the inhabitants of the earth, whose names have not been written in the book of life from the foundation of the world, will be amazed when they see the beast, because it was and is not and is to come.' In other words, it appeared in the past, disappears at times and then appears once again. This seems to mean the power of the beast can be eliminated, but it will reappear at different times.

When the Roman Empire was overthrown, the power of the beast reappeared in different forms. When the Tsar was assassinated in Russia, injustice was not overthrown. Eventually Stalin emerged who was worse than any of the Tsars. The head of one tyrant is chopped off and people think they are rid of him, but he reappears in a different form and people are astonished. Those who don't understand that Jesus Christ is Lord of all the earth are amazed and impressed.

❏ *What does Babylon the prostitute do?*
Babylon the prostitute is sitting on the beast, but she is not the beast. Verse 4 says: 'The woman was clothed in purple and scarlet, and adorned with gold and jewels and pearls, holding in her hand a golden cup full of abominations and the impurities of her fornication.' She is beautiful, with diamonds just dripping off her! And beautifully dressed. Very alluring. The beast represses people, but the prostitute seduces. And they work together against us! Hendriksen comments: 'The symbol indicates that which allures, tempts, seduces and draws people away from God.'[2]

For over forty years, Christians in Eastern Europe were repressed by the beast. We haven't realised it but, in the Western world, we have been seduced by the prostitute. There was nothing seductive about Eastern European communism — virtually everybody was trying to get away from it. But in escaping from that beast, people in Eastern Europe get seduced by the values of the West.

What seduces people? Money, sex and power. These things have made it difficult for people in the Western world to become followers of Jesus. The prostitute of Babylon, it seems to me, is quite simply seduction. If the devil cannot succeed with persecution through the beast, he will try seduction. While he has tried all round the world to persecute Christians, he has largely failed. Persecution seems to do good things to Christians — it makes them strong.

But seduction does bad things to Christians. When we look at the Western world over the last few decades, we can see that we have been seduced to the point that the church in the West is weak and powerless. Many churches now have hardly anyone in them. They are just small gatherings of old folk waiting for the end to come. The church in the West has been seduced by the values of the prostitute. By money, sex, and power.

There's a terrible warning here. Babylon is a seducer and the values of the system are all around us. 'Come out from it!' That is the impassioned prophetic cry. It comes from Isaiah 52, verse 11 and it refers to the return from Babylon. Don't get sucked into the values of Babylon. It's a prostitute and it will destroy you. It will take away your faith and all the things that are precious to you.

❏ *Who are the seven kings?*
We are given an insight into the meaning of this passage in verses 9 to 11: 'This calls for a mind that has wisdom: the seven heads are seven mountains on which the woman is seated; also, they are seven kings, of whom five have fallen, one is living and the other has not yet come; and when he comes, he must remain only a little while.' Most commentators see in the seven mountains (verse 9) a reference to Rome. This is the place where the woman sits. Rome was the place through which the beast and the harlot exercised their influence. But Rome was not the limit of their influence. The vision speaks of kings extending to both the past and the future.

There are various ways of looking at this. Some people interpret the seven kings as seven emperors in Rome. Others see them as seven kingdoms beginning prior to this time and extending through into the modern era. The number seven, in Revelation, is a symbol of completeness, of totality, and it seems to me more likely that this passage is saying that kings come and kings go, but the power of the beast lives on as part of our present human experience.

❏ *Who are the ten future kings?*

Then we read about ten future kings: 'And the ten horns that you saw are ten kings who have not yet received a kingdom, but they are to receive authority as kings for one hour, together with the beast' (verse 12). A few years ago, Hal Lindsay wrote a book in which he said the ten kings were the ten nations of the European Economic Community.[3] This interpretation points up the danger of identifying these visions too closely with particular historical incidents, as there are now more than ten nations in the European Community!

We are told in verse 7 that this is a mystery. When we see the word 'mystery', we think it means a detective mystery — a 'whodunit'. And so we think we have to identify the ten kings. But the Bible uses this word in quite a different way. After Jesus had taught the people using parables, the disciples went to him and said, 'We can't understand you.' His reply was: 'To you it has been given to know the mysteries of the kingdom of heaven, but to them it has not been given' (Matthew 13, verse 11).

The apostle Paul wrote of the need to understand 'the mystery of Christ. In former generations this mystery was not made known to humankind, as it has now been revealed to his holy apostles and prophets by the Spirit: that is, the Gentiles have become fellow heirs, members of the same body, and sharers in the promise in Christ Jesus through the gospel' (Ephesians 3, verses 4 to 6). So it does not mean a mystery in the sense of having to look for all the clues. It means a revelation of great truth.

We are told that the ten kings represent future kingdoms that will hold power for brief periods. The ten kings are rulers who give their power to the beast. The beast, through these ten kings, will make war against the Lamb and, as we have seen, there will be a final conflict between the forces of good and evil, light and darkness. Finally, God will triumph, the powers of darkness will be overthrown and God's kingdom will be established.

❏ *What is the final outcome?*
At the end of this section, in verses 16 and 17, an interesting thing happens: '. . .and the ten horns that you saw, they and the beast will hate the whore; they will make her desolate and naked; they will devour her flesh and burn her up with fire. For God has put it into their hearts to carry out his purpose by agreeing to give their kingdom to the beast, until the words of God will be fulfilled.'

At the end of time, the evil powers that are at work on the earth — the prostitute and the beast — end up fighting each other, because it is in the nature of evil to self-destruct. Finally, there comes the moment when history, as we know it, comes to an end. The prostitute is burned up, the beast is destroyed and God reigns.

Billy Graham tells a story he heard in the former

USSR when he visited there during the Cold War years:

> After the Bolshevik revolution, the local communist leader had been sent to tell the people the virtues of communism and to take their minds away from religion, which Karl Marx called 'the opium of the people'. After the communist had harangued them for a long time, he said to the local Christian pastor rather contemptuously: 'I will give you five minutes to reply.'
>
> The pastor replied: 'I do not need five minutes, only five seconds.' He rose to the platform and gave the Easter greeting: 'The Lord is risen!' As one, the villagers thundered back: 'He is risen indeed!'[4]

The tyrants of this world will come and they will go. Stalin thought he would control the destiny of the world and where is he now? Hitler said he would change the course of history for a thousand years and where is he? Honeker put up the Berlin Wall and said it would last for a hundred years and where is he? The tyrants come and go, but one person finally will rule — Jesus Christ, the Son of the Living God, the King of kings and the Lord of lords.

The fall of Babylon
(chapter 18, verses 1 to 24)
Now we see the fall of Babylon the Great City (verse 2). As she falls, the world's economic systems fall with her. 'We miss the point of it all if we conclude with many modern critics that John is concerned only to denounce contemporary Rome,' says Leon Morris. '[John] is thinking not of the fall of one city or empire, but of the collapse of civilisation. Final judgment means the overthrow of all that opposes itself to God.'[5]

This is the second part of the vision of Babylon the prostitute. Why the great city? Historically, economic power has been concentrated in the city.

❑ *The 'great city' in the past*
The economic centre of the world in which the early Christians lived was Rome. Two hundred years ago, it was London — the heart of the world's largest empire which, it can be argued in the biblical sense, was Babylon.

The glories of the British Empire were largely built on the slave trade — in many instances built on appalling acts of injustice and oppression in the colonies. It took Christian leaders like William Wilberforce to stand against the powerful who had built the British Empire. We can thank God for men and women down through history who did not project the prophetic call for justice into the future but who, realising that the message was for their time, acted.

❏ The 'great city' today

And today? I think anyone who writes on Revelation needs to do so with a certain hesitancy, bearing in mind how many people have been proved wrong with the passage of time. But two very significant things are happening in cities around the world today. First, we are seeing the urbanisation of the earth, as increasing numbers of people move into cities.

Second, in the last few decades, we have seen a revolution in technology. The great cities of the world are linked today in a way people could never have anticipated before. There is a sense in which the great cities of the world are becoming economically and technologically one city. If there is a hiccup on the New York Stock Exchange, a few hours later, when Tokyo opens, the effects are felt — and then people wonder what will happen when London opens.

In 1989, TIME magazine produced a report illustrating what is happening today within the world's economic system. The article said that in South America, the richest twenty per cent of the population live an extravagent lifestyle, more affluent than the rich in any of the wealthy nations of the world. Alongside that, in most of South America, between sixty and eighty per cent of the population are living in situations approaching the despair of famine-stricken Africa or Bangladesh.

In 1989, the inflation rate in Argentina was 3 500 per cent and the richest twenty per cent were investing their money offshore, which meant their resources were not being used for the benefit of their own countries. Rich Latin Americans have more money invested in the United States, says TIME, than the total foreign debt of the three biggest nations in South America — Brazil, Argentina and Mexico. So, in Latin America, phenomenal wealth is owned by a small percentage of the population who live in opulence, while the masses are living in increasing poverty.[6]

Even in many Western nations, which are supposed to illustrate the success of capitalism, the gap between the rich and the poor is growing wider.

❑ *God's view of our economic systems*
But what does God think of our economic systems? We are given a few clues in the Old Testament where he laid down some provisions for the people of Israel. He gave them several holidays that expressed his views on economics. The most important one came every fifty years, when the Year of Jubilee was to be celebrated. Slaves were to be freed, all debts cancelled and all land returned to its original owners (Leviticus 25). In an agricultural society, land is wealth. Over a period of time, wealth tends to accumulate into the hands of a few, so God's provision was that every fifty years the trumpet was

to be blown on the system and the land was to go back to the original owners.

However, there is some debate among scholars whether the Year of Jubilee was ever celebrated, the general consensus being that it was not. It is not hard to understand why. After fifty years, if someone has the power and owns the trumpet, he is not going to blow it and see all he has accumulated given back to the poor! People will find all sorts of reasons why the land should not go back to the poor and why slaves should not be freed.

What can be done about injustice? Karl Marx devised an economic theory based on political justice. At the expense of human liberty, his solution was to wipe out the rich and powerful and redistribute the wealth. But the result was an economically stagnant totalitarian nightmare from which people fled as soon as they were able.

So what will God do about these economic systems? The answer is that he will overthrow them. Babylon has become 'a dwelling place of demons' and 'all the nations have drunk of the wine of the wrath of her fornication' (verses 2 and 3). In verse 4 to 8, there is a call to the people of God in the midst of this unjust system. The call is this: 'Come out of her, my people, so that you will not share in her sins.'

John was echoing the call of the Old Testament prophets. After the people had been taken captive into Babylon, there came a point when the prophets said the time was fulfilled, the time for deliverance had come and it was now time to get out of Babylon. How do we get out of a system when it surrounds us all the time? We don't buy into its values — and the values of Babylon are money, sex and power.

Then destruction falls on Babylon. All those who benefited from Babylon gather around and cry, 'Woe' (verse 10). The kings of the earth have lost their luxuries and power, and they are terrified at the torment of Babylon. All the merchants can do is weep because no-one wants to buy their luxury items. They dealt in the same commodities that clothed the prostitute (chapter 17, verse 4), and in the bodies and souls of people (verse 13). There were sixty million slaves in the Roman Empire and they were traded like commodities. Those who had grown wealthy from the transportation and distribution industries stand there and weep and mourn. In one hour, all their work and dreams have been taken from them.

Suddenly in verse 20, we hear a prophetic cry: 'Rejoice over her, O heaven, you saints and apostles and prophets! For God has given judgment for you against her.' And a mighty angel pronounces death to the city — like a millstone thrown into the ocean never to be seen again.

We are reading about the most revolutionary message the world has ever heard. It is far more powerful than what Karl Marx propounded. The message is that God has taken sides with the victims of Babylon — the persecuted, the weak, the poor, the exploited and the abused.

In the meantime, until God finally acts at the end of history, the followers of Jesus are called to take sides with God against the false values of Babylon — all her harlotries, her money, her sex and her power. We are to stand with the persecuted, the weak, the poor, the oppressed and those who are ripped off by Babylon and her values. God does hear the cry of the weak and the oppressed of the earth and one day he will act.

The wedding banquet
(chapter 19, verses 1 to 10)

The first ten verses of Revelation 19 conclude the extended vision about Babylon, the symbol for the systems of the world organised against the values of God. Babylon has been overthrown and the rejoicing begins. From heaven comes the roar of a multitude shouting one word, 'Hallelujah!'

This word is found in the New Testament only here and it appears four times. 'Hallelu' means praise; 'jah' is short for Yahweh. The people in heaven on this final day have seen God's purposes finally fulfilled and they begin shouting in triumph, exhorting each other to begin praising the Lord. The oppressors of the weak and the poor of the earth have finally been overthrown and God has triumphed.

What is our picture of heaven? What is our picture of God's victory at the end of history? The picture here is of a wedding banquet, with festivities and celebration. We are invited to the marriage supper of God. We are told that the bridegroom is the Lamb and the bride is his followers.

In the New Testament, marriage is often used as a picture for the relationship between Christ and ourselves. It helps if we understand something of ancient Jewish marriage, because it was different from our own.

There were four stages. The first was betrothal when the announcement was made of the forthcoming wedding. It was a more legally binding relationship than our engagement, although similar to it. The betrothal was followed by the payment of the bride price. A man wanting to marry had to have enough goods to go to the woman's father and, after bartering with him, give him the agreed brideprice. Then came the great day of the wedding. The groom went with his friends to the home of the bride without announcing the time of his arrival. There they were joined together in marriage. The fourth stage, the festivities, began and these could go on for as long as a week.[7]

We find this picture of the wedding used as an illustration all through the Bible. It begins with the announcement of betrothal in the Old Testament. The prophets said there would come a day when God would come and pledge himself in love to his people. Then came the payment of the bride-price:

> From heaven he came and sought her
> to be his holy bride.
> With his own blood he bought her
> And for her life he died.[8]

Then on the final day, Jesus will come with his friends, unannounced, to claim the bride. We are told he will come back with the holy angels, and then the festivities will begin. We can put away our watches, because it won't go on for two hours or a week; it will continue through all eternity. It will be a celebration of the final victory of God and the achievement of his purposes throughout the earth. And we are invited.

What will I wear? Who else is going? They are the sorts of questions we ask when we get a wedding invitation. We are told in verses 7 and 8 we will wear fine linen, bright and clean. The fine linen stands for the righteous acts of the saints. This doesn't mean St Peter and St Paul. It's a New Testament term for all who follow Jesus.

Then I think: 'Horrors! I will have to go threadbare if the only way I can be at God's final celebration is through my own righteous deeds.' Why did John say that? Did he not read the letters of Paul, that it is all of grace?

The answer is that righteousness, our being right with God, is a gift. This beautiful garment we are given to wear on the final day at the marriage celebration is not something made *by* us — it is something made *for* us. Every act of righteousness we do throughout our lives is a work of God's grace. An old hymn says: 'Every virtue we possess and every victory won, and every thought of holiness are his alone.'[9] If we could sit at sewing machines till kingdom come, we could never by our own deeds make this beautiful garment. It has been made by Christ and he, by his grace, is the one who enables righteous deeds to be done. It is not our righteousness but his, working through our lives by his grace and mercy.

This understanding of grace is very important to everyone who wants to take the prophetic call for justice seriously. In our zeal to call for repentance, it is very easy to sound like we are offering a new law — if only people will behave in a certain way, they will be acceptable to God. Rather the message arises from grace and is about grace from beginning to end. Even our acts of repentance are brought about by the grace of God.

Jesus liked stories about weddings. There was one he told about a man who organised a wedding banquet and all sorts of people came in response to his invitation. It was a parable of the gospel — that all are invited to come and follow Jesus. Then Jesus went on to tell what happened to one man who was not wearing the wedding garment — a gatecrasher who wanted to go to the party, but who was not prepared to go on the king's terms. He turned up in his old clothes and he stood out because everyone else was wearing beautiful clean wedding garments. The king was really upset and tossed the fellow out (Matthew 22, verses 11 to 14).

Jesus is saying that the invitation to join in the final celebration of God's victory is open to all, but we cannot go on our own terms. There's a garment we have to be prepared to put on. Either we are clothed with the righteousness of Christ or we are unclean.

This is a strange kind of wedding because the only person invited is the bride! 'And the angel said to me, "Write this: Blessed are those who are invited to the marriage supper of the Lamb"' (verse 9). Who are they?

In Luke's Gospel, we read another story Jesus told about a banquet. 'Someone gave a great dinner and invited many. At the time for the dinner he sent his slave to say to those who had been invited, "Come, for everything is now ready." But they all alike began to make excuses. . . So the slave returned and reported this to his master. . . who said to his slave, "Go out at once into the streets and lanes of the town and bring in the poor, the crippled, the blind and the lame'" (Luke 14, verses 16 to 21).

The Bible is a book about mission on every page! The invitation went out and the people to whom it was given could not be bothered and made excuses. So God said, 'I know who will respond. It will be the poor, the despised, the lame, the crippled, the people who are nobodies in the eyes of others — they will respond to my invitation.'

That mission spirit is at the heart of God's nature. We are called to respond to his purposes and give out the invitations. Not simply to think, 'when the roll is called up yonder, I'll be there,' but to realise the Father has a guest list. It will be made up of those people who are aware of their spiritual poverty and who are ready to respond to God's invitation. Right to the end, the message of the Bible is a call to mission.

Discussion questions

Talking it through

1 Using the material in chapter 17, verses 1 to 18, how do you feel the differing roles of the beast and Babylon the whore operate?

2 Do you see the purpose of the woman on the beast image in chapter 17 as primarily a warning or an encouragement?

3 What, precisely, is the nature of the evil of Babylon as outlined in chaper 18? Do you feel that the punishment is justified?

4 How does the picture of Jewish marriage help you understand in a fresh way the nature of our possible relationship with God?

146/The system that seduces the world

Widening our horizons

1 From your own particular perspective, what institutions that you know have characteristics of Babylon the whore on the one hand and the beast on the other, and indicate as precisely as you can what those characteristics are. Does this exercise help you in any way — for example, to know the nature and power of sin?

2 American Christian psychotherapist Richard Foster has written a book called *Money, Sex and Power*. How can the three be tied up in people's minds to form a tantalising, seductive mix that leads us into sin?

Create a short fiction/factual story that shows these three tied up on any *one* of these themes:
(a) a high-flyer in the business world
(b) a dealer in the international drug scene
(c) an apparatchik in the former Soviet Union
(d) a talent scout on the international sports circuit.

3 'The city is not itself evil, but concentrated humanity means concentrated everything, both good and evil.' How can each of the following city-type institutions be used for evil:
   (a) The stock exchange?
   (b) The city government?
   (c) The urban real estate industry?
   (d) The financial sector?
   What can be done about such evil?

4 Assume you are limited in no way — by tradition, by any other than your own wish — in what elements you would include in a marriage ceremony. What elements do you feel are essential and why?

6
The final horseman

REVELATION CHAPTER 19, VERSE 11 TO
CHAPTER 20, VERSE 15

THE SENSE OF AN APPROACHING CLIMAX emerges in this section, beginning with the rider on the white horse and leading to the final judgment.

The rider on the white horse (chapter 19, verses 11 to 21)
The fifth horseman of the apocalypse appears: 'His eyes are like a flame of fire, and on his head are many diadems; and he has a name inscribed that no-one knows but himself. He is clothed in a robe dipped in blood, and his name is called the Word of God. . . On his robe and on his thigh he has a name inscribed, "King of kings and Lord of lords"' (verses 12, 13 and 16).

There is no debate as to the identity of this horseman. This is Jesus the Lord. He has ridden out, is dressed for battle and ready to fight the first four horsemen of the apocalypse. As deception, war, famine and death enslave the peoples of the earth, King Jesus rides out to do battle and we, as followers of Jesus, take sides. We are called to be engaged with Jesus in the struggle against these four scourges as they ravage the earth. Wilcock points out that although some speak of Jesus riding forth to his last battle in the vision, the text itself does not speak of what he 'is going to do, but what he is: conquering king, righteous judge, captain of the armies of heaven'.[1]

It has been said that, in many cases, the evangelical branch of the church today is preaching a gospel of individual personal conversion that does not call people to engagement with the things which are ravaging the earth.[2] It seldom challenges people to stand on the side of the poor and the weak and the oppressed, whatever that may mean for us in our own individual circumstances. It will obviously be different for each person, but this is the cry of the biblical Jesus and the radical challenge of the book of Revelation. The fifth horseman has ridden out to do battle with the forces of oppression and darkness; we have to decide where we will stand.

Then an angel announces what one commentator

has called 'a macabre parody of the invitation to the other banquet'.[3] He calls out to the vultures to feast on the powerful of the earth who have exploited the poor and persecuted the godly (verses 17 and 18). Then the rider on the white horse engages all the powers of darkness that have oppressed, persecuted and destroyed. Into the fire are thrown the beast who, right through history, has demanded of people allegiance that belongs only to God; the false prophet who has deceived people; and all the forces of evil that have ravaged the earth. They are all defeated (verses 19 to 21). Some events in the book of Revelation we can see unfolding down through history. But these events mark the end.

In 1989, soon after South African President F.W. de Klerk relaxed the laws on public gatherings, thousands of people came together to demonstrate against apartheid. One gathering was led by a group of Christians which included many ministers. A television interviewer asked the Anglican Archbishop of Cape Town, Desmond Tutu, 'Isn't this situation hopeless?' He replied, 'No.' Cynically the interviewer asked, 'How can you possibly have hope in this situation?' Tutu said, 'Because I follow a man who was put to death on a Friday and came back to life on a Sunday — and that gives me hope in the struggle.'

Do we really believe it? Are we prepared to follow the call of the biblical Jesus? Or are we part of the church that has short-changed the gospel of Christ because we have not understood the greatness of God's calling to his people? The early Christians facing persecution and death were given a powerful picture of the King who rides out to engage the forces of injustice and oppression. It is a picture that can challenge us to do likewise.

The thousand years
(chapter 20, verses 1 to 6)

In a parody on the reign of Jesus Christ, Adolf Hitler said that the Third Reich would last for a thousand years. This thousand-year reign is referred to as the millennium. This thousand-year reign of Christ has a very big place in some people's thinking about the second coming.

❏ *What are we to understand by the thousand years?*

Previously we have seen the beast and the false prophet thrown into the lake of fire. As this next part of the vision starts, Satan gets bound and Christ reigns for a thousand years. There are two ways we may understand this:

The first is that we have here a chronological sequence of events. This view has been widely taught over the past century. In its most popular form, this viewpoint has become almost a touchstone of orthodoxy in some evangelical communities in the United States. According to this view, first Jesus comes back and takes out of the world all those who are his followers. Then, during a seven-year period, the events of the book of Revelation occur. This is based on a particular interpretation of Daniel 9. At the end of that time, Jesus comes back again and reigns on earth for a thousand years. Following that period, he defeats Satan and fully establishes his kingdom.

One problem with this way of understanding Revelation is that the rest of the Bible knows of one second coming, not two or three. Another problem is that, in this view, the events of Revelation are seen to relate solely to an 'end time' period. Thus they would have had no immediate relevance to those who first read the book.

The other option which we have been following is to see Revelation as a series of visions which overlap. It is a message to the early church and to the people of God throughout history. It is a prophetic call to be aligned with the purpose of God in the world.

For the early Christians who were worshipping in the catacombs and in caves and being put to death, this letter from John filled their hearts with hope. This book got into the Christian canon of scripture, not because it referred to a hypothetical seven-year period at the end of time, but because it is a message inspired by the Holy Spirit to bring hope to the people of God. And it can bring hope today.

When John writes about the dragon, serpent, bottomless pit and chain, it is obviously symbolic. If we are to chain Satan, we don't go and get a metal chain with a padlock! One writer insists that the chain was meant literally because nothing is too hard for God. While it is true that God can do anything, the writer has missed the point.[4] If the dragon, serpent, bottomless pit and chain are symbolic, should the thousand years be taken literally? My understanding is that, as this is a vision and what is being described here is symbolic, then the thousand years would also be a symbol. It is part of the language of vision.

Interestingly, the term 'a thousand years' is used in one other place to refer to the second coming (2 Peter 3, verse 8). There, it is also used symbolically to speak of the long period of time between Jesus' first and second comings.

❏ *What is to happen during the thousand years?*
The first thing that happens during this thousand-year period is that Satan is bound. In another place in the New Testament, we find this particular expression. Jesus said: 'But no-one can enter a strong man's house and plunder his property without first tying up the strong man; then indeed the house can be plundered' (Mark 3, verse 27). Jesus was talking about the devil and saying that he could not be

overcome unless someone stronger came and bound him. Satan was bound at the cross where, we are told, the rulers and authorities were disarmed and Jesus triumphed over them (Colossians 2, verse 15).

Yet though bound, Satan obviously still has a great deal of power. William Hendriksen makes this comment:

> . . .the devil is not bound in every sense. His influence is not completely destroyed. On the contrary, within the sphere in which Satan is permitted to exert his influence for evil, he rages most furiously. A dog securely bound with a long and heavy chain can do great damage within the circle of his imprisonment. Outside that circle, however, the animal can do no damage and can hurt no-one.[5]

We are told in this vision the purpose of the binding is to keep the dragon — Satan — from deceiving the nations (verse 3). This poses a serious problem. As we look around the world today, it is manifestly obvious that the nations are deceived.

So what does the Bible actually say about the nations of the world? If we go back to the beginning and look at the calling of Abraham, we find that God called him so 'all the families of the earth shall be blessed' (Genesis 2, verse 3). God's purpose was that the nations would no longer be deceived, but would come into the light of the truth of God.

Tragically, the Old Testament is the story of the failure of Israel to fulfil this mandate. Instead of the people of Israel following what had been given to Abraham, they kept the message to themselves with the result that the nations remained deceived, living in darkness. Then Jesus came. As a baby he was taken to the Temple where he was met by Simeon, who had been waiting because the Lord had told him he would see the Messiah. He prophesied over the baby and said: 'Master, now you are dismissing your servant in peace, according to your word; for my eyes have seen your salvation, which you have prepared in the presence of all peoples, a light for revelation to the Gentiles' (Luke 2, verses 29 to 32). From the start, the purpose of Jesus' coming was that the nations could be led out of deception into the light.

When Jesus sent out the seventy, he told them to proclaim the kingdom of God. So they went and healed the sick, cast out demons, and said: '. . .the kingdom of God has come near you' (Luke 10, verse 9). When they returned to Jesus, he said: 'I watched Satan fall from heaven' (Luke 10, verse 18). Satan was defeated. How? Through the power of the gospel in the work of Jesus.

A very significant point in Jesus' ministry came as he arrived in Jerusalem for the last time. A group of Gentiles went to one of the disciples and said: 'We wish to see Jesus.' His reply on hearing this request was: 'Now is the judgment of this world; now the ruler of this world will be driven out' (John 12, verses 21, 31 and 32). Jesus was going to the cross where Satan, the prince of the world, would be overcome and defeated. In his final discourse to his disciples, when speaking to them about the nations, Jesus said: 'And this good news of the kingdom will be proclaimed throughout the world, as a testimony to all the nations; and then the end will come' (Matthew 24, verse 14).

If we want to interpret the book of Revelation, we must go back to the Old Testament, the Gospels and the New Testament letters. A symbolic passage of scripture needs to be interpreted by the literal passages of scripture, not vice versa. We get ourselves into trouble if we start with the symbolic, visionary parts and then interpret the rest of scripture in that light.

The binding and the defeat of Satan are often mentioned through the Gospels. Satan is overcome by the entrance of Jesus into this world. Satan is bound through the preaching of the gospel, Satan is defeated through Jesus going to the cross, and the powers of darkness are destroyed by the resurrection of Jesus from the dead. We read that, as the good news is proclaimed throughout the earth, the nations who live in darkness will come into the light. And this is what John is saying in this vision — that during the time between Christ's first coming to earth and his return, Satan is bound, so the nations can come out of deception and into the light of the gospel.

We sing songs like 'Jesus is Lord of all the earth, he is the King of creation'[6] — but do we believe it? Some seem to believe that Satan is lord of all the earth and there is little we can do about the terrible things that happen.

But the light does break through the deceptions under which the nations suffer. We saw one example during the momentous events of 1989 that occurred in Eastern Europe. When Gorbachev met John Paul II, TIME magazine said,'The czar of world atheism meets the vicar of Christ. This meeting of the Pope and Gorbachev symbolised the end of the twentieth century's most dramatic spiritual war. Until recently, the battalions of Marxism seemed to have had the upper hand over the soldiers of the cross.'[7]

Before he became Pope, John Paul predicted that, as an ideology, communism would soon stand for nothing except the perpetuation of power. As an economic system, he said, it had failed. He also predicted that, within a short time, Marxism as a force would be finished within the Eastern block countries and that, as communism collapsed, there would be a huge turning to Christianity.

In the nine months between March and November 1989, three thousand new churches were opened in the Soviet Union. In October 1989, for the first time since the 1917 Revolution, a Christian worship service was held inside the Kremlin. The Bible said Jesus came to earth to take people out of darkness into light and it is happening in the world today. We don't have to wait for some period in the future.

This is a call for us to be involved in sharing the gospel now. The nations of the world are in darkness. They are deceived. But Satan has been bound by Christ. So, as the gospel is proclaimed, as every new believer steps out of darkness into light, the darkness is pushed back that much further.

A great Japanese Christian, Kagawa, once said that the reason the early Christians triumphed over pagan Rome was because they out-thought, outlived and outdied the pagans. This happened in Eastern Europe. Leaders in the Protestant churches in East Germany, the Catholic churches in Poland and in some of the Orthodox churches in Russia have out-thought the Marxists, and they have outlived the Marxists morally and ethically. The czars of East German communism lived secretly in unbelievable opulence while they preached socialism and equality for all; it was an amazing betrayal of an ideal.

And the Christians outdied the Marxists. Fifty thousand priests in the Russian Orthodox Church were estimated to have been put to death between 1917 and the time Krushchev finished leading the Soviet Union. But the light was never extinguished.

And where the light penetrates, the nations can no long totally exist in darkness.

The early Christians reading this letter understood this. Satan had been bound, the nations of the world needed no longer to be deceived, the gospel was spreading and their friends who had been persecuted and died were in heaven reigning with Christ (verses 4 to 6). Truly, a message of great hope.

The defeat of Satan
(chapter 20, verses 7 to 10)

At the end of this reign of Christ, we encounter the final onslaught of evil, when the powers of darkness rise up for their final fling. The nations of the earth are described as 'Gog and Magog' (verse 8), a picture drawn from a prophecy in Ezekiel 38, verse 2. They are deceived by Satan and readied for the final battle.

In one of his letters, Paul says: 'Let no-one deceive you in any way; for that day will not come unless the rebellion comes first and the lawless one is revealed, the one destined for destruction... And you know what is now restraining him, so that he may be revealed when his time comes. For the mystery of lawlessness is already at work, but only until the one who now restrains it is removed' (2 Thessalonians 2, verses 3, 6 and 7). Although scholars debate who or what 'restrains' evil, there does seem to be a real parallel between this passage and Revelation 20, verses 7 to 10.

In other words, there is a force restraining evil in the world today, because the enemy was overcome at the cross. There will come a time when that restraint will be removed. Then will occur the final cataclysmic showdown that we saw in Revelation 16 — the Battle of Armageddon — when the devil and Jesus Christ engage each other. The devil is conquered and thrown into the lake of burning sulfur, where the beast and the false prophet had already been thrown. The end comes quickly. It is plainly the intervention of God. The devil and all those systems he has used for his evil purposes finally stand under the judgment of God.

Without the assurance of this final victory we would wonder if we lived in a moral universe. Evil seems so often to triumph. But here is the prophetic word: God will act in justice; the devil himself will finally be subject to the eternal judgment of God.

The final judgment
(chapter 20, verses 11 to 15)

Then John sees a vision of the final judgment with a great white throne and books being opened. One book is called the Book of Life containing the names of all those who are the followers of Jesus. God judges everyone according to what is written in the books.

Jesus said: 'When the Son of Man comes in his

glory, and all the angels with him, then he will sit on the throne of his glory. All the nations will be gathered before him, and he will separate people one from another as a shepherd separates the sheep from the goats, and he will put the sheep at his right hand and the goats at the left. Then the king will say to those at his right hand, "Come, you that are blessed by my Father, inherit the kingdom prepared for you from the foundation of the world; for I was hungry and you gave me food, I was thirsty and you gave me something to drink, I was a stranger and you welcomed me, I was naked and you gave me clothing, I was sick and you took care of me, I was in prison and you visited me.". . . Then he will say to those at his left hand, "You that are accursed, depart from me into the eternal fire prepared for the devil and his angels"' (Matthew 25, verses 31 to 41).

What words of encouragement to the small groups of persecuted followers of Jesus in the first century! God can be trusted, and he will judge justly. But what awful words of warning to those whose names are not found in 'the book of life', who reject God's love and mercy and live in rebellion to him. Ahead of them is a 'second death' — eternal separation from the presence of God. But it does not have to be like this. God has entered our humanity in the person of his Son, that we might turn from our sinfulness and find eternal life through him.

Discussion questions

Talking it through

1 Chapter 19, verses 17 to 21 is particularly gruesome. Why do you feel the writer paints such a macabre scene?

2 Using chapter 20, verses 1 to 6, indicate how powerful God is on the one hand and the devil on the other. How does this explain our conflicts between good and evil?

3 What specific points of hope are there in chapters 19 and 20?

4 What contribution does chapter 20, verses 11 to 14 make to our understanding of who is accountable for sin? In the light of this, how would you explain the role of the devil in your own sinfulness?

Widening our horizons

1 Precisely what 'powers of darkness' would you see at work in each of these situations:
  (a) the racial problems in South Africa
  (b) the poverty problems in Third World megacities
  (c) the malnutrition in the Horn of Africa?

2 How can a belief that 'God never changes' and that 'God is trustworthy' be encouraging when we look at the following:
  (a) the collapse of ancient Roman atheism?
  (b) the collapse of Fascism and atheism?
  (c) the decay of Soviet and East European atheistic communism?

How does what followed each of these show, however, that 'humankind does *not* get better and better'?

3 Many Jews today are 'secular Jews' — that is, they don't believe in God — and this, in many cases, arises from the experience of the Holocaust. How can Christians respond to such horrifying events, given the picture we have in Revelation 19 and 20? What would you say to a Jew in such a situation?

4 In what ways are you aware of the sort of conflict between good and evil described in these chapters:
(a) in your own life?
(b) in that of someone of your acquaintance?
(c) in the society around us?

7
Beyond the end of time

REVELATION CHAPTER 21, VERSE 1 TO
CHAPTER 22, VERSE 1

IN CHAPTER 21, JOHN IS TRYING TO DESCRIBE events and realities which are indescribable, so we need a vivid imagination to understand what he is saying. He is writing about life beyond time itself, to the time when this world will have ended, beyond God's final judgment on humanity.

It is a little like listening to someone from a very remote part of the world confronted for the first time in his life with an example of advanced technology such as an aeroplane. Such a person would have great difficulty describing it, because they would not have the technological words to explain what it is.

The description would not necessarily be wrong, but would sound very inadequate to people with greater technological knowledge. John is describing the new universe and he has to describe it in terms that his readers would be familiar with, but he is really trying to describe the indescribable.

The writings of C.S. Lewis are of great help here. The final book in the Narnia series is called *The Last Battle*. It concludes:

> . . .but the things that began to happen after that were so great and beautiful, that I cannot write them. And for us, this is the end of all the stories and we can most truly say that they all lived happily ever after. But for them it was only the beginning of the real story. All their life in this world, and all their adventures in Narnia, had only been the cover and the title page: now, at last, they were beginning chapter one of the great story which no-one on earth has read, which goes on for ever, in which every chapter is better than the one before.[1]

C.S. Lewis' *Voyage to Venus* is a science fiction story in which a man named Ransom goes to the planet Venus. At the end of the book, there is a discussion about the end of their world. Ransom is talking with Tor the King:

> 'And that,' said Ransom, 'will be the end?' And

Tor the King stared at him. 'The end?' he said, 'Who spoke of an end?' 'The end of your world, I mean,' said Ransom.

'Splendour of heaven!' said Tor. 'Your thoughts are unlike ours. About that time we shall not be far from the beginning of all things. . .'

And Ransom said, 'But what you call the beginning, we are accustomed to call the last things.'

'I do not call it a beginning,' said Tor the King. 'It is but the wiping out of a false start in order that the world may then begin. As when a man lies down to sleep, if he finds a twisted root under his shoulder he will change his place — and after that his real sleep begins. Or as a man setting foot on an island may make a false step. He steadies himself and, after that, his journey begins. You would not call that steadying of himself a last thing?'

'And is the whole story of my race no more than this?' said Ransom.[2]

Lewis is saying that this history of humanity, from the moment when we sinned against God, has been, from God's perspective, one false step on a journey in the wrong direction, and that's all. God corrects the mistake that has been made and the real journey begins. In *Voyage to Venus*, Lewis calls it 'the great dance' and he has an amazing picture of a celebration going on through the vastness of the universe. John begins to see just the tiniest glimpse of eternity's 'great dance'.

The real story is about to begin — and we are told almost nothing about it! Here, and in one or two other places in the Bible, God has given us just a glimpse, because that is all we need to know.

The new Jerusalem
(chapter 21, verse 1 to chapter 22, verse 6)

John sees a 'new heaven and a new earth. . . I saw the holy city, the new Jerusalem, coming down out of heaven from God' (verses 1 and 2). He begins to see a remarkable, holy, new city — and it is beautiful. And the only way John can think of to describe it is to say that it is like a bride dressed up for her husband.

Then, we have one of the most beautiful passages in the Bible. I have often stood at a graveside and read these words. 'And I heard a loud voice from the throne saying, "See, the home of God is among mortals. He will dwell with them as their God; they will be his people, and God himself will be with them; he will wipe every tear from their eyes. Death will be no more; mourning and crying and pain will be no more, for the first things have passed away"' (verses 3 and 4).

'And the one who was seated on the throne said, "See, I am making all things new." Also he said, "Write this, for these words are trustworthy and true." Then he said to me, "It is done! I am the Alpha and the Omega, the beginning and the end.

To the thirsty, I will give water as a gift from the spring of the water of life"' (verses 5 and 6). This is John's picture of the new universe. He sees the new heaven and earth as a city — the new city of Jerusalem that comes from God, the heavenly Jerusalem where God dwells.

But the people who cannot get into it are the citizens of Babylon — 'the cowardly, the faithless, the polluted, the murderers, the fornicators, the sorcerers, the idolators, and all liars; their place will be in the lake that burns with fire and sulphur' (verse 8). That is where Babylon was cast and this is the second death.

John's initial view of the holy city coming down out of heaven in verse 2 was from a distant vantage point, but now in verse 10 the Spirit shows him the city in more detail. With great surprise, we learn that the city is a cube! Not only is it a cube, but it is vast! It is 2 200 kilometres in every direction — about the size of the moon if it were cubed (verse 16). What are we to make of a symbol like this?

There is symbolism in the measurement which is lost in English translation. We are told in the Greek text that the measurement of the cube is 12 000 stadia (2 200 kilometres) in each direction. If all the edges of the cube were measured, the total measurement would be 12 x 12 000 stadia = 144 000. This is the symbol for the people of God we met in the vision in chapter seven of Revelation.

Martin Luther King said that the new city which God is building is not an unbalanced entity with caring virtues on one side and degrading vices on the other but, in its completeness, is an expression of the length and the breadth and the height of the character of God. It is vast. It is immeasurable. It is absolutely beyond our understanding.[3]

Then, John sees right into the city. There is no temple, no sun, no lamp, no night. The gates are never shut and there is no sin. Flowing through the centre is a river and along its banks is the tree of life (chapter 22, verses 1 and 2). The story of Adam and Eve sinning and being driven out of the garden, indicates that they no longer had access to the tree of life. But here we find that all we have been denied through history because our ancestors sinned and turned away from God will one day become ours again. Paradise will be regained and God will be there! The river will bring life and the leaves of the tree will be for the healing of the nations.

So the end of the Bible is linked right back to its beginning, when God created man and woman and put them in paradise where there was a river and the tree of life (Genesis 2, verses 9 and 10). But Adam and Eve took one false step and the history of the human race has been a tragedy of missing the mark of God's purpose for us ever since — a story of war, murder, death and the exploitation of the weak. What good there has been through history is because the image of God within us has never been totally erased.

Here — at what we call the end, but which possibly God hardly even regards as the beginning — everything is reversed and we are back at the beginning. It is no longer a paradise garden for two people. Now it is a city for the uncountable multitudes who are there to worship God. The throne of the Lamb is in the city and a river is flowing through it. This river appears in many places in the Bible. It starts off in the Garden of Eden; in Psalm 46, verse 4 we read: 'There is a river whose streams make glad the city of God.' Ezekiel had a vision of the river that flowed out of the temple and it brought life and healing (Ezekiel 47, verses 1 to 12).

As John begins to describe some of the characteristics of this city, we make a very interesting discovery — nearly all the descriptions are true of the people of God today. First, the city is called a bride (verse 9), a common picture for the church of Jesus Christ. Second, the city has gates and written on them are the names of the twelve tribes of Israel (verse 12). The New Testament tells us that there is continuity of the people of God right through the Old Covenant into the New. And the city is built on the foundation of the apostles (verse 14). The apostle Paul also tells us that the church is built upon the foundation of the apostles and prophets and Christ is the cornerstone (Ephesians 2, verses 19 and 20).

Then, we discover that there is no temple in the city (verse 22). Under the old covenant there had to be a temple, but in the new covenant that came with Jesus Christ there is no need because the Holy Spirit has come to dwell in those who have put their faith in Jesus. The light of the city comes from Christ — and this is true for us today as well. The gates of the city are never shut: the striking thing about the gospel of Jesus Christ is that it is offered to all peoples.

One gate faces north, one south, one east and one west. The message of the Gospel is open to people of all cultures. But 'nothing unclean will enter it, nor anyone who practices abomination or falsehood, but only those who are written in the Lamb's book of life' (verse 27). How do we get into this city? We become citizens by acknowledging Jesus as Lord.

When the Romans established a colony in Philippi, Thessalonica or wherever, they introduced Roman customs, Roman law and the Roman language. When someone went to one of these Roman colonies, they could look around and see people in togas and hear them speaking Latin, and could say, 'This is a foretaste of being in Rome!' In the same way, followers of Jesus are to embody to the world today what life in the world to come will be like. A person encountering a group of Jesus' followers should be able to say, 'This is what heaven will be like!' There are some things reserved for the future, like the immediacy of the presence of the Lamb, and no more tears. But many of the amazing characteristics of this city can equally be descriptions of those who are the followers of the Lamb.

I believe this is the message for us. It isn't just about an indescribable future. It is about the church that God is calling us to be now. Tragically, we can instead spend our lives speculating about the furniture of heaven and the temperature of hell. It doesn't have to be like that, though. We have an exciting life we are called to live — a lifestyle which is a foretaste of heaven itself.

Come to Jesus!
(chapter 22, verses 6 to 21)
John has finished trying to describe the indescribable — life in another dimension. The kingdom of God has come and, in this chapter, he writes a postscript to his letter. The 'P.S.' is a plea which says quite simply, 'Come to Jesus.'

God has shown him what lies ahead for humanity and John ends it by writing: 'The Spirit and the bride say, "Come." And let everyone who hears say, "Come." And let everyone who is thirsty come. Let anyone who wishes take the water of life as a gift' (verse 17).

174/Beyond the end of time

❑ *Why we should come to Jesus (verses 6 to 16)*
John states five reasons for our coming to Jesus:

(a) We should come to Jesus because the message is true.
'And he said to me, "these words are trustworthy and true"' (verse 6). As we have looked at the book of Revelation, we have discovered things that characterise the age between Jesus' first coming to earth and when he returns. We saw four horsemen riding around the world: deception, war, famine and death. We then saw that the environment would be impacted and partly destroyed.

Then a beast appeared who was a representation of regimes that demand allegiance that belongs only to God. The beast was slain, but he reappeared. We met Babylon the whore, who seduced people with the values of the world.

Finally, we saw Jerusalem, the holy city, coming down from God and we heard the invitation to become citizens of the kingdom of God. The message that John received from God made sense of the world John lived in, although it came to him in vivid pictures. It makes sense of the world in which we live in a way that no other ideology does.

(b) We should come to Jesus because he is coming back again.
Jesus said, 'See, I am coming soon!' (verse 7). But can Jesus not tell the time? Peter addresses this concern in his second letter: 'First of all you must

understand this, that in the last days scoffers will come, scoffing and indulging their own lusts and saying, "Where is the promise of his coming? For ever since our ancestors died, all things continue as they were from the beginning of creation!" But do not ignore this one fact, beloved, that with the Lord one day is like a thousand years, and a thousand years are like one day. The Lord is not slow about his promises, as some think of slowness, but is patient with you, not wanting any to perish, but all to come to repentance. But, in accordance with his promise, we wait for new heavens and a new earth, where righteousness is at home' (2 Peter 3, verses 3, 4, 8, 9 and 13).

Peter is saying Jesus' return hadn't happened as quickly as one would expect. But there is a reason why — God is patient with humanity. Jesus also said: 'This good news of the kingdom will be proclaimed as a testimony to all the nations; and then the end will come' (Matthew 24, verse 14).

We don't know whether the kingdom might have come before now if, over the centuries, the people of God had grasped the message of Jesus and taken it to the whole earth. But we do know that we are living on borrowed time. Jesus said the reason for his delay is to give people an opportunity to repent and come to him.

(c) We should come to Jesus because he is the only one who deserves to be worshipped.

'I am the Alpha and the Omega, the first and the last, the beginning and the end,' Jesus states in verse 13. An angel had been showing John all the amazing things that would happen through human history and, hardly surprisingly, John had fallen down to worship him. But he was told not to (verses 8 and 9).

The apostles of Jesus experienced similar reactions. The apostle Peter once entered a group of people and a man fell down on his knees. Peter took hold of him and said, 'Stand up; I am only a mortal' (Acts 10, verse 26). Every great religious leader has had similar reactions. When people tried to worship the Buddha, he said not to, but to seek the truth. When people tried to worship Mohammed, he said not to worship him, but only Allah. Only Jesus, of all the world's great religious leaders, accepted worship. When people started worshipping him, he didn't say, 'Don't do it.'

(d) We should come to Jesus because he will be judge of all the earth.
'My reward is with me, to repay according to everyone's work' (verse 12). We find a very strange verse here. 'Let the evildoer still do evil, and the filthy still be filthy, and the righteous still do right, and the holy still be holy' (verse 11). Is Jesus saying that, if we're bad, we might as well continue being bad; and if we're good, we might as well continue being good? That's certainly contrary to what he

said elsewhere!

But we use this word 'let' in two different ways. We use it as an exhortation: 'Let's do this.' Or we use it by way of resignation: 'Let it be.' I think this second sense is what is meant here. If we have heard the call to follow Jesus, but have said 'No' to the love of God, then let it be.

In the context of this book, looking at the whole of eternity, this is a very sober thing Jesus is saying. If we want to do wrong in this world then, on the other side of death, we will continue doing wrong. If we choose to do what is right here then, on the other side of death, we will continue doing right. Jesus will be judge of all the earth and we are given a choice. The way we live here on earth will determine our eternal destiny.

(e) We should come to Jesus because he is the one who cleanses from sin.
'Blessed are those who wash their robes, so that they will have the right to the tree of life and may enter the city by the gates' (verse 14). It is as though every one of us has a robe which is our character. Everything we do throughout our lives is woven into this. Every thought, word and deed goes into this character. No human detergent can get it clean. Only the shed blood of Christ can make it clean. Only those who are washed clean by Jesus, not by any good deeds of their own, can enter the city.

Outside the city are other people, who are called

by various names. The first group are called 'the dogs'. This is not a bunch of friendly, smiling puppies wagging their tails. In the ancient world, dogs used to run round the streets like rats do today. These are the people who practise magic arts, who are into occultism and the powers of darkness, those who are sexually immoral, those who are murderers, whose lives are filled with hatred, and those who love and practise falsehood.

There are many like that today. At the end of the day it is not God who excludes anyone. We exclude ourselves if we choose a lifestyle contrary to the values of the kingdom of God.

❏ *The invitation to come (verse 17)*
'The Spirit and the bride say, "Come!"' (verse 17). We know how God's Spirit invites us to come to Jesus. It happens in various ways. When we sin, we feel miserable. The Spirit is prompting us to come to Jesus, to find his forgiveness and cleansing. Sometimes we experience an inner stirring and a kind of aspiration that, surely, there is more to life than what we are experiencing. That's the Holy Spirit. He is saying to us 'Come!'

And the bride, too, says 'Come!' We often hear stories of people who meet a group of Christians and sense these people have something they don't. That's the bride saying 'Come!' 'Let everyone who hears say, "Come!"' That is the person who has heard the gospel and believed, calling others. Who may come to Jesus? 'And let everyone who is thirsty, come. And let everyone who wishes take the water of life as a gift' (verse 17). Jesus once sat down at a well and asked a woman who was drawing water if she would give him a drink. Then he said to her that while whoever drank that water would be thirsty again, whoever drank the water he gave would never be thirsty. The woman said to him, 'Sir, give me this water,' and Jesus replied, 'Go, call your husband and come back' (John 4, verses 4 to 18). Jesus put his finger on the one area in her life that would need to change if she were going to follow him.

It is God who puts an inner thirst within our lives for reality, meaning and hope. The message of the Bible is that only Jesus can satisfy that longing for meaning. Riches cannot, knowledge cannot and drugs cannot satisfy it.

Who may come? Whoever wishes. What is offered to us is a free gift.

But we are all suspicious when we hear about amazing free gifts. We wonder what the catch is. But if we are to know God, it can only be a free gift! There's no other possible way and we are only ready to receive this gift when we can see our own need and say, 'God, I have sinned against you. I know I cannot be good enough to earn your forgiveness.' Then, we find to our amazement that God has reached out to us. This is what the life of

Jesus is all about. God came and lived among us and said, 'I love you — I want to reach out to you in love. Here is the gift of my forgiveness; now accept it.'

Revelation ends with a warning not to tamper with the message (verses 18 and 19). But this happens all the time. People say, 'All these bits about the righteousness of God — I don't believe that.' Or, 'This whole deal about a life of sexual purity — that doesn't feel right to me.' Coming to Jesus is not a 'multiple-choice' package — taking the nice bits, but rejecting the challenge to my lifestyle by refusing to acknowledge the justice of God and his concern for the poor. We are told here that we tamper with the message at our peril. We either receive it, or we reject it.

But how do we keep going once we have accepted the message? John ends his letter with this comment: 'The grace of the Lord Jesus be with all the saints' (verse 21). That's how! It is not through our own efforts. It is not a case of thinking, 'Oh dear! How can I get through today, doing all those things I'm supposed to do as a Christian?' It is not like that; it is about receiving God's grace as a gift.

The revelation has ended. God has given John a series of visions of the future of the human race. We are left with the challenge of placing our trust in Jesus, the one who alone holds the key to human destiny.

Discussion questions

Talking it through

1 What qualities are we meant to see the city as having in chapter 21, verse 1 to chapter 22, verse 6?

2 What features of the original Garden of Eden do we find mentioned in chapter 21? Why is there such a similarity between the new Jerusalem and Eden?

3 While the heavenly city is a vision of the future, much that is described in chapter 21 can be 'fingerprints' of our being destined for that future. What aspects mentioned here can't we expect to implement?

4 What does the time delay in the coming of Jesus tell us about what God is like?

5 What are the details of the message of God referred to in verses 18 and 19 that cannot be tampered with? Why is this warning included? How do you think John can justify such a statement?

Widening your horizons

1 If we are to look at the story of humanity on earth from God's perspective, how would it look, do you think? Create a picture in your imagination that helps explain it and that takes into account:
(a) the multi-dimensional character of eternity
(b) the limited dimension of earth.

2 There is no temple in heaven because of the presence of God (verse 22). Does this knowledge affect your attitude to the apparently 'fixed assets' of church today — buildings, church government, church organisations?

3 What is your vision of the future? To what extent does it correspond to the one Jesus offers in chapter 22? What questions for you does the vision in chapter 22 leave unanswered? Why are all these questions not answered?

4 What do you believe eternity is going to be like? To what extent do you believe we are going to retain our individuality, our idiosyncrasies? Do you believe choice is going to continue to play a part? How important to you are answers to these questions? Is there anything frightening about this?

5 What evidence of 'eternity' do you see in your own life? Do you have a longing for it? Do you see that longing as a sense of belonging? What does that longing tell you about God?

Endnotes

Introduction
1. William Barclay, *The Revelation of John*, Vol.I, The Saint Andrew Press, 1959, p.1
2. Philip Carrington, in William Barclay, *op.cit.*, p.2
3. G.R. Beasley-Murray, *The Book of Revelation*, Oliphants, 1974, p.16

Chapter 1
1. Stephen Hawking, *A Brief History of Time*, Bantam, 1988, p.184
2. C.S. Lewis, *Reflections on the Psalms*, Fontana, 1958, pp.78-83
3. Michael Wilcock, *I Saw Heaven Opened*, Inter Varsity Press, 1975, p.85
4. Billy Graham, *Approaching Hoofbeats*, Hodder and Stoughton, 1983, p.163
5. *Ibid*, p.164
6. *The Government That Will Bring Paradise*, Watch Tower Bible and Tract Society, 1985, p.15
7. William Barclay, *The Revelation of John*, Vol.2, The Saint Andrew Press, 1959, p.29
8. *Ibid*, p.45

9. In Walter B. Knight, *Master Book of New Illustrations*, Eerdmans, 1956, p.160

Chapter 2
1. William Hendriksen, *More than Conquerors*, The Tyndale Press, 1940, p.116
2. Leon Morris, *Revelation*, Inter Varsity Press, 1987
3. Lynn White, in Francis A. Schaeffer, *Pollution and the Death of Man*, Tyndale House, 1970, pp.97-115
   Francis Schaeffer, *op.cit.*, p.10
4. Michael Wilcock, op.cit., p.92
5. Francis Schaeffer, *op.cit.*, p.10
6. *Christchurch Star*, 24 October 1990
7. Michael Wilcock, *op.cit.*, p.94
8. David Barrett, *World Christian Encyclopedia*, 1991 statistics.
9. William Barclay, *op.cit.*,Vol.2, p.83-85
10. Leon Morris, *op.cit.*, p.147

Chapter 3
1. Michael Wilcock, *op.cit.*, pp.110–114
2. Leon Morris, *op.cit.*, p.152
3. Oscar Cullmann, *Christ and Time*, SCM, 1951, p.84
4. William Barclay, *op.cit.*, p.103
5. Eusebius, *The Ecclesiastical History*, 3.5
6. William Hendriksen, *op.cit.*, p.145
7. Michael Wilcock, *op.cit.*, p.131
8. *Ibid*, p.132
9. For example, Tim LaHaye, *Revelation Illustrated and Made Plain*, Zondervan, 1973, pp.75–77
10. G.R. Beasley-Murray, *op.cit.*, p.224

Chapter 4
1. For example, the understanding of history we find in Isaiah 45

2. Michael Wilcock, *op.cit.*, p.149

Chapter 5
1. Tim LaHaye, *op.cit.*, pp.230–237
2. William Hendriksen, *op.cit.*, p.167
3. Hal Lindsay, *The Late Great Planet Earth*, Zondervan, 1970, pp.92–97
4. Billy Graham, *World Aflame*, World's Work, 1965, p.133
5. Leon Morris, *op.cit.*, pp.207–208
6. 'A Chasm of Misery', *TIME* magazine, 6 November 1989, pp.46–48
7. William Hendricksen, *op.cit.*, pp.179–180
8. 'The Church's One Foundation', Samuel John Stone, 1939–1900
9. 'Our Blest Redeemer', Henriette Auber, 1973–1862

Chapter 6
1. Michael Wilcock, *op.cit.*, p.183
2. Jim Wallis, *The Call to Conversion*, Lion, 1981, p.xiv
3. Michael Wilcock, *op.cit.*, p.185
4. Tim LaHaye, *op.cit.*, p.278
5. William Hendrikson, *op.cit.*, p.190
6. Donald Fishel, 'Alleluia, Alleluia, Give thanks to the risen Lord', 1973
7. 'Cross meets Kremlin', *TIME* magazine, 4 December 1989, pp.50–52

Chapter 7
1. C.S. Lewis, *The Last Battle*, Puffin, 1964, p.165
2. C.S. Lewis, *Voyage to Venus*, Pan, 1953, pp.196–197
3. Martin Luther King, in Garth Hewitt, *Nero's Watching Video*, Hodder and Stoughton, 1987, p.20

Bibliography

Useful commentaries on Revelation

Barclay, William, *The Revelation of John*, St Andrew Press, 1959
A commentary with considerable background material, taking the approach that the text relates largely to the first century world.

Beasley-Murray, G.R., *The Book of Revelation*, Oliphants, 1974
A scholarly commentary with particular emphasis on the relationship of Revelation to other apocalyptic writing.

Fiorenza, E.S., *The Book of Revelation, Justice and Judgement*, Fortress, 1985
A learned but well-written work which not only explains the text satisfactorily, but also covers the secondary literature on the book.

Hendriksen, William, *More than Conquerors*, Tyndale Press, 1940
A commentary seeking to relate the sequential visions of Revelation to the events of the first century and to subsequent history.

LaHaye, Tim, *Revelation Illustrated and Made Plain*, Zonderman, 1973

Typical of the popular 'end times' commentaries that see the events of Revelation relating to a seven-year period at the end.

Morris, Leon, *Revelation*, Inter Varsity Press, 1987
A good verse-by-verse exegesis of the text. An update of an older work.

Wilcock, Michael, *I Saw Heaven Opened*, Inter Varsity Press, 1975
A commentary that sees the prophetic message of Revelation as a series of overlapping visions relating to past, present and future.

Useful treatments of key ideas in Revelation

INTERPRETATION

Fee, G.D. and Stuart, D., *How to Read the Bible For All It's Worth*, Zondervan, 1982
Chapter 13 deals with the issues involved in interpreting Revelation.

Goldworthy, G., *The Gospel in Revelation*, Paternoster, 1986
Looks at Revelation from the central theme of the gospel of Jesus Christ.

Mounce, R.H., *The Book of Revelation*, Eerdmans, 1977
A collection of essays on Revelation, interpreting it in its historical context of first century Jewish apocalyptic, expressing the experience of those who were powerless.

THEOLOGY

Guthrie, D., *New Testament Theology*, Inter Varsity Press, 1981
Part 8, 'The Future', deals with this theme throughout the New Testament, including sections on Revelation.

Ladd, G., *A Theology of the New Testament*, Eerdmans, 1974

APOCALYPTIC

Russell, D.S., *Apocalyptic: Ancient and Modern*, SCM, 1978 and Morris, L., *Apocalyptic*, Eerdmans, 1972
Both books deal with the nature of apocalyptic belief and the literature expressing it.

ESCHATOLOGY

A Guide to Biblical Prophecy, Armerding, C.E./Ward Gasque, W. (eds), Hendricksen, 1989

The Meaning of the Millennium: Four Views, Clouse, R.G. (ed) Inter Varsity Press, 1984

Grenz, S.J., *The Millennial Maze*, Inter Varsity Press, 1992

Ladd, G.E., *Crucial Questions concerning the Kingdom of God*, Eerdmans, 1956

Ladd, G.E., *The Blessed Hope*, Eerdmans, 1956

Ladd, G.E., *The Last Things*, Eerdmans, 1961

Travis, S.H., *I Believe in the Second Coming of Jesus*, Hodder, 1982

Williams, D.J., *The Promise of His Coming*, Lancer, 1990

Useful treatments of present-day faith-and-life issues raised in Revelation

WORSHIP

Webber, Robert, *Worship is a Verb*, Word, 1985
An evangelical discovers the strengths of the liturgical tradition and the charismatic experience.

SPIRITUAL CONFLICT

Wink, Walter, *Naming the Powers*, Fortress, 1984

Wink, Walter, *Unmasking the Powers*, Fortress, 1986

Wink, Walter, *Engaging the Powers*, Fortress, 1992
A significant series of books addressing the question of how we are to understand 'the powers' today, both in their biblical content and in relation to the contemporary struggle.

McAlpine, Thomas, *Facing the Powers*, MARC, 1991
A look at Reformed, Anabaptist, Charismatic and sociological understanding of the powers.

JUSTICE AND THE GOSPEL

McCloughry, Roy, *The Eye of the Needle*, Inter Varsity Press, 1990
A call to the church to be a witness to God's kingdom of justice and love.

Scott, Waldman, *Bring Forth Justice*, Eerdmans, 1980
An evangelical rediscovers the dimension of justice in the gospel.

Stott, John, *Issues Facing Christians Today*, Marshalls, 1984
A wide-ranging discussion on the values of the gospel and many of the major issues facing us today.

Sugden, Christopher, *Racial discipleship*, Marshalls, 1981
The gospel and its challenges to a range of justice issues.

Wallis, Jim, *The Call to Conversion*, Lion, 1981
A call to personal conversion that will engage issues facing the world.

PERSECUTION

Shenk, C.S., *When Kingdoms Clash*, Herald, 1988
The Christian in the face of totalitarian ideologies.

ECONOMICS

Owensby, Walter, *Economics for Prophets*, Eerdmans, 1988
A helpful introduction to economic theory from a biblical perspective.

Sider, Ron, *Rich Christians in an Age of Hunger*, Hodder & Stoughton, 1977
The challenge of global inequalities.

Yoder, John Howard, *The Politics of Jesus*, Eerdmans, 1972
Jesus' approach to 'jubilee' economics, among other things.

CITIES

Bakke, Ray, *The Urban Christian*, IVP, 1987
The challenge cities pose for the gospel.

Grigg, Viv, *Companion to the Poor*, Albatross, 1984
How can the gospel be made meaningful among the poor of the world's mega-cities?

Grigg, Viv, *Cry of the Urban Poor*, MARC, 1992
The need for a wholistic gospel to face the huge challenges of the urban poor.

THE FUTURE

Graham, Billy, *Approaching Hoofbeats*, Hodder & Stoughton, 1983
Relates the four horsemen of Revelation to the issues of deception, war, famine and death.

Sine, Tom, *Wild Hope*, Word, 1991
A call to wake up; to the big issues facing the world and the church.